The Loveliest Story Ever Told

The Revd Murdoch Campbell, 1957

The Loveliest Story Ever Told

Murdoch Campbell

Edited by David Campbell

Covenanters Press

Covenanters Press
an imprint of
Zeticula Ltd,
Unit 13,
196 Rose Street,
Edinburgh,
EH2 4AT,
Scotland.

http://www.covenanters.co.uk
admin@covenanters.co.uk

First published September 1962
Reprinted December 1962
Reprinted February 1963

This edition published 2016
Text © David Campbell 2016

Front cover: *Cottage Interior, Glen Esk* © Copyright George
    Paul Chalmers
Back: *Rannoch Moor* © Copyright Horatio McCulloch RSA

ISBN 978-1-905022-34-2

Acknowledgements

Thanks to Derek Prescott for generously carrying out photographic work.

Thanks also to my wife Evie Campbell for her encouragement, comments and forbearance.

Resolis Free Church Manse

Preface

THIS little work is meant primarily for the young who are so much exposed in these times to ideas and influences which can only deepen their misery and lead them further away from the path of true happiness.

Within the framework of a familiar Biblical story I have tried to show that, properly understood, the Gospel of Christ alone provides us with the key to an understanding of our relationship to God, of our deep spiritual needs and of the only way which leads to true and lasting happiness and peace.

The story, however, should make its appeal to all —both young and old— who value the blessings of the Gospel.

My use of illustration and anecdote should, I hope, help to elucidate certain points which, within the context of modern theological works, some of the younger readers may not easily follow.

It is, indeed, with a deep prayerful concern for the everlasting welfare of everyone who may read this book that I have tried to tell a little of "what God hath wrought".

Murdoch Campbell
Resolis, Conon, Ross-shire, 1962

Mrs Campbell with collie

Contents

1

"The Loveliest Story Ever Told"

What led me into the English class-room that afternoon I cannot now recall, for English was not one of my subjects. When I entered, the room was full and the famous Professor —Sir Herbert Grierson of Edinburgh University— was about to deliver his ordinary lecture for the day. Of all that he said during that hour I can now remember nothing apart from the few unforgettable words which throughout the years have remained in my memory with unfading clarity. "Perhaps the loveliest and the most perfect story ever told is to be found in the Bible —in Genesis Chapter twenty-four; it is the story of Abraham's servant in his quest for a bride for his master's son."

These, as nearly as I can now recall them, were his words. Even now, and for that one moment, I seem to see the man and to hear his voice. Also, I seem to see the intent and somewhat surprised look on the faces of his numerous students as they listened to his words. And down through the years that one brief scene and saying have haunted my imagination like a pleasant dream. I cannot tell how often I have read that familiar Biblical story since that day, but, the more I read it, the more I am impressed with its idyllic beauty and spiritual significance.

The sheer literary grace of the story is, of course, all unconscious. As its quiet drama unfolds our emotions are, somehow, touched at their deepest level. It is a story which brings us into touch with the quiet pastoral word of a bygone age. Its human tenderness and pathos, its atmosphere of devotion and, above all, the deep love which moves at its very heart, make us realise how wonderful and noble life may be if we are blessed by the same influences and are in touch with the same living streams. For this also is a story in which we may see both the love of God and the finger of God.

1

The story begins with an old man sitting in his tent in Hebron. He had seen many and eventful years. His wife, his companion in his joys and sorrows, now lies in her grave near an oak tree at Machpelah. He knows that the God Who had been his Friend and Companion in the way would soon gather him also to his people. Now that his pilgrimage on earth is about to close, the future welfare of his well-beloved son is giving him concern. He is still unmarried and he is anxious that he should now have someone who would worthily share his life and love, along with the great and far-reaching blessings and promises which God had, in such an awe-inspiring manner, confined to himself and to succeeding generations down through the ages to come. These promises were related to the salvation of the world through the Blessed One who, according to the flesh, was to descend from his family and Who would appear in this world in a future age. It was through this Person, this 'Angel of the Covenant', that he saw through the vistas of prophetic time the glorious destiny of his spiritual seed.

As he muses on all this, a prayerful resolution forms in his mind. He would call his well-trusted servant —probably Eliezer— and send him forth to the far country of his own kindred. There God might have someone ready to share his son's life along with his great spiritual inheritance.

And the servant is worthy of his master's trust. Aware of the importance and significance of his mission, he turns at once to God for guidance and good success. After selecting priceless jewels and costly robes —for his master and his son were very rich —he went forward with prayer on his lips that God might prosper his journey and show him a sign for good.

As the cavalcade of camels with their riders moved through the silent desert, and as night after night the stars beamed out of the evening sky, this faithful servant continued praying to God. And when at last the long journey between Hebron and Haran was nearly over he knew that the hour was big with destiny.

Arriving at the well outside the city at the time when 'women go out to draw water', he offered an audible prayer to

God. "And he said, O Lord God of my master Abraham I pray thee, send me good speed this day, and shew kindness unto my master Abraham. Behold, I stand here by the well of water, and the daughters of the men of the city come out to draw water. And let it come to pass that the damsel to whom I shall say, Let down thy pitcher, I pray thee, that I may drink: and she shall say, Drink, and I will give thy camels drink also: let the same be she that thou hast appointed for thy servant Isaac; and thereby shall I know that thou hast shewed kindness unto my master." This was his prayer. This was the sign he asked of God who had guided him in the way.

It was a sign that was calculated to throw much light on the character and disposition of the girl worthy of his master's son. He was merely to ask her for 'a sip' —as the Hebrew word may be rendered— of water for himself only; but the one whom God had chosen to be the mother of a great people and a remote ancestress of Jesus Christ would reveal her generous nature and her willingness to serve others by offering him not a mere 'sip' of water but an abundant 'drink'. To this she was also to add the astonishing offer of drawing water for the camels also. Now when we consider that those ten beasts, after the toil of the long desert, were prepared to empty at least four barrels of water in all, the spontaneous willingness of the girl of his prayers to serve man and beast would point to a kindly and an unselfish disposition and also to a character of the highest order.

How beautifully does the finger of God move in this story. While the servant was still praying that God would give him this sign, there appeared at his side a young woman who 'was very fair to look upon'. She was a girl whose physical and moral life was one of loveliness and purity. With exquisite grace and bearing she spoke and acted as he had prayed to God she would. God truly had answered his prayer in a way that filled him with wonder. At that moment he knew that, as Abraham had promised, God had sent His Angel before him. That sure and invisible guide had truly led him in 'the right way'.

His thankfulness to God for giving him such a clear sign of His favour he could only show in an act of kindness towards the fair but still unknown 'daughter' who stood beside him. In giving her two golden bracelets and an earring of gold he asked the question —'Whose daughter art thou, and is there room in thy father's house for us to lodge in?' Again there fell from her kindly lips words of assurance that all the company were welcome to share in the hospitalities of her home. And the disclosure that she was a near relative of Abraham made him bow his head once more in prayer, while the bejewelled and astonished girl went home to tell her family about the impressive stranger who had asked her for a drink.

That evening as the stars reappeared in the clear Oriental sky, the company sat down in her father's spacious tent where the servant told them how God prospered his master and of his purpose in coming so far. He told them too of the unmistakeable signs of God's guidance. But he must not tarry. Their answer, whether Yes or No, must be given at once. His master was waiting, and God's business demanded haste and an immediate decision.

Rebecca's father and brother could not but consent that God was very intimately present in all the events which led up to this decisive hour. "The thing proceeds from the Lord: Behold, Rebecca is before thee, take her, and go, and let her be thy master's son's wife, as the Lord hath spoken." This was the hour for which the pious servant had prayed.

The immediate effect on his spirit was that of profound thankfulness to God, and in the presence of all the company he bowed himself to the earth and worshipped God. To seal the covenant between them, and as the first tokens of her great inheritance, he brought forth jewels and goodly raiment which he handed to the girl whom God had so greatly honoured. Gifts of gold were also given to her brother and mother. These were meant to commemorate and seal the happy transaction on which God had smiled. A feast of joy followed. And the rest of that night, as the company lay down to sleep, must have been rendered very peaceful through a deep sense of God's presence.

4

As the servant awoke he could not but think of Abraham whom he had left in far-away Hebron. He knew that in the shade of those trees 'where he called on the name of the Lord' his worthy and well-beloved master would sometimes turn his eyes toward the distant plain for some sign of their return. He would therefore depart at once that his master also might rejoice in knowing how his prayers had prevailed with God.

It was at this moment that a dark unlooked-for cloud descended on the servant's joyous soul. Both Rebecca's mother and brother demanded that she should remain with them for 'a few days, at the least ten'. Here was something like procrastination, if not opposition. Ten days! Truly some evil spirit had instilled this thought into the minds of her loved ones! It was an hour of crisis which could only be solved by Rebecca herself. 'We will call the damsel and inquire at her mouth.' And there, standing near those whom she loved and to whom she was so attached by the ties of nature, she was asked the one question which was to determine her earthly happiness, if not her everlasting destiny. 'Wilt thou go with this man?' As the decisive question was put to her we wonder if she paused. Did she bow her head in silent prayer? Did she blush as a tear struggled to escape her eyelids? We cannot tell. All we know is that, like the chime of a distant bell, the brief, irrevocable reply fell from her lips: 'I will go'. And as they moved away toward the land of her choice she bade an everlasting farewell to her people and kindred.

It would be unreasonable to think that Rebecca had a full and immediate grasp of all that was involved in her decision and calling. As yet she just stood on the threshold of a life the wonder of which she could hardly grasp. From that moment her name took on the colour of immortality. By one word she stepped forward into history, for her name, her life and her faith were now perpetuated in God's everlasting Word. From that moment her higher relationship to God also entitled her to privileges, honours and blessings which she could, as yet, but dimly apprehend.

The long journey towards the south is now nearly over. The eyes of Rebecca are alive with interest as the kindly hills of the south come into view —the scene of her future home! And in one of the nearer fields a man may be seen walking. It is her future husband, wistfully waiting for the cavalcade which his keen eyes may have seen coming over the crest of the hill an hour before. As they come near, and as the servant recognises his master's son, Rebecca dismounts, and out of deep respect for the one whose life she was now to share, she covers her face with a veil. Isaac had no difficulty in recognising her, for did she not wear on her person the costly jewels and robes which he had sent her? In that hour an undying love for each other was born in their hearts, a love which sustained them in after days through all the trials which they were called upon to endure.

This story, as it is written down in the Bible by the pen of inspiration, is truly 'lovely', but whether Sir Herbert had any appreciation of its spiritual and higher meaning one cannot tell. It is, in fact, a story which has given beauty and vividness to a lovelier story by far —the story of God's love towards the sinful children of men. Indeed the whole story is deeply symbolic and instructive; for it illustrates in a wonderful way the mysterious love of God Who from all eternity decreed that His Son also should have a Bride —one who should share His love and inheritance throughout the ages to come. It is, under the guise of a lovely type, the story of the heavenly marriage of Christ and His Bride.

One does not need to apologise for giving the story this spiritual meaning and elevation. The Scriptures permit this since they, also, use this very symbolism of marriage as eminently fitted to portray the covenant relationship between Christ and His people. In the Forty-fifth Psalm, for example, we have a lovely portrayal of Christ, the Bridegroom, and His Bride, the Church. There we see them both enframed within the same divine song. The respective and peculiar glories of each are minutely described. Their love for one another, or the eternal union between them, is that which gives depth and dignity to this exquisite Psalm. There, within the glorious transactions of God's grace, we see them brought together on earth till they pass outwith our view into their eternal home.

Perhaps the book in the Bible where this symbolism reaches a height of perfection is the *Song of Solomon*. To the devout Israelite this book was 'the holy of holies' of divine revelation; and throughout the Christian centuries many choice Christians have also found in this book the secrets of a divine and holy love the knowledge of which is for ever hidden from, and beyond the spiritual reach of, all to whom God is a stranger.

And lest any should say that such a symbolism is a mere 'oriental extravagance' which is not inherent in the Gospel we may look into the New Testament to see it there also, and in words of even deeper tenderness and meaning. When John the Baptist would bring the incarnate Lord and His people face to face he exclaimed in ecstasy: 'He that hath the bride is the bridegroom'. As he saw one of the great transactions of the eternal world now brought to its fulfilment in time, his own joy was unspeakable.

Our Lord's parable of the marriage of the king's son is also to be understood within the meaning of this symbolism. He is the king's Son whose marriage calls for an outflow of God's loving-kindness toward men. To celebrate this great event a feast of unending joy is prepared for all who are willing to come.

We never perform a marriage ceremony without reading the wonderful words which show the ideal standards which should grace and govern Christian marriage. "Husbands, love your wives, even as Christ also loved the church, and gave Himself for it: that He might sanctify and cleanse it with the washing of water by the word: that He might present it to Himself a glorious church, not having spot, or wrinkle, or any such thing. .. This is a great mystery: but I speak concerning Christ and the church." In these words we see this symbolism given a practical significance within both the temporal and the divine order.

The last words in the Bible speak of this same love and relationship. 'The marriage of the Lamb is come, and His wife hath made herself ready.' The tenderness and kindness which dwell in her Lord's heart we find in her heart also. Her last word to us from the threshold of her heavenly home is 'Come'.

Our story is therefore one that is consistent with Scriptural usage. It is, as we shall see, one that has often provided many preachers of the Gospel with rich spiritual material which makes the theme of God's grace both winsome and endearing, as well as one of infinite consolation to the people of God. It also makes the Gospel theme intelligible to all levels of mental capacity and spiritual apprehension.

It is a great pity, therefore, that some have complicated this lovely emblem of God's covenant relationship with His people. Within a strange mode of interpretation they make a distinction between the Church and the Bride. With the Bible in our hands, however, are these not one and the same? Christ's own answer to this question is: 'My dove, my undefiled is but *one*'. And it is the story of His love for His Bride that we now wish to tell.

2

God's Son and Heir

The Bible as we know is, primarily, a perfect revelation of God's grace. It is a glass through which we may look into the very heart and mind of God. It is a mirror which reflects His glory. It is, among other things, God's letter of love to His Church. It reveals the near and dear relationship in which Christ stands to her. It is a voice which tells us of the unfolding mysteries of the eternal world.

It tells, us, for example, that God has one Son by eternal generation, and that this Son is the perfect image of Himself. He is His equal in power and glory. This Son is, therefore, in a different category of existence from all other sons. All others enjoy a place in God"s family by an act of grace; through a spiritual rebirth and a loving adoption.

The Scriptures also tell us that this Son is God's Heir. As Isaac became the heir of the great spiritual and temporal inheritance which his father received from God in a covenant, so Christ is 'the heir of all things'. The phrase 'all things' is inclusive of everything in the universe and beyond it. Both the world of glory and the universe which lies within time and space belong to Christ. His possessions and riches are, therefore, unsearchable. 'The Father loves the Son, and has given all things into His hand.' But His real riches are spiritual, heavenly and eternal.

These riches, however, were not to be confined to Him only. They were given to Him that He might share them for ever and ever with a countless number whom God had loved but whom sin had impoverished and slain. Christ, in fact, had willed that His Bride should share in all His riches.

Another wonder of divine revelation is that God had decreed that His Son should be married. This is the 'great mystery' of which Paul speaks, and which moves at the very heart of Scriptural revelation. Long before the earth was formed, God decreed that since He loved so many of the children of men He should therefore give them to Christ in a covenant. They were given to Him that He might redeem them to God, and so have fitness to occupy His glorious palace in the eternal world. Christ Himself tells us that God for this very purpose had given them to Him. 'They were yours, and you gave them to me.'

Among men, for example, it is sometimes customary that on her wedding day the bride should be given away to her future husband by her father. This act of surrender does not, of course, affect her father's love for her in any way. Because he loves his daughter he is willing that she should enter into a new relationship which might lend greater dignity and honour to her life. In the same way God gave away His own people to Christ so that within a new relationship they might be both redeemed and raised into a state of inconceivable dignity and honour.

In the Scottish Highlands there was once a famous preacher —the Rev. Francis MacBean of Fort Augustus— who used to comment in the pulpit on this theme. He would speak of that 'hour' when it was made known to 'the principalities and powers in the heavenly places' that the Son of God, by His Father's decree, was to take to Himself a Bride. Such tidings would have filled the heavenly world with astonishment —that the Great God should bring any of His creatures, however holy and exalted, into such a relationship with Himself. But when the news resounded throughout the upper world of glory that the subjects of God's special choice and love were men and women belonging to a fallen race, the mystery of God's love began to deepen beyond their comprehension. This, indeed, is one of the things which angels and men shall desire to look into throughout eternal ages, but the mystery of God's sovereign love and choice is too great and too deep for finite minds to fathom.

Another glorious aspect of divine revelation, therefore, is that the heart of Christ was engaged in love to His Church from all eternity. 'I have loved thee with an everlasting love.' 'Having loved His own which were in the world, He loved them unto the end.'

Within the circle of human experience there are, we know, those who fall in love, and who could tell when their affections first rested on certain persons. Perhaps they could also tell why they ceased to love those who once claimed their heart in all its tenderness and devotion. It may be that their love cooled and died because those who once commanded their love 'let them down'. They became involved in some scandal or shame, and fell far beneath the moral dignity and social level which they should have maintained. Therefore they disown them for ever. Human love, in other words, is liable to change and even to die. It has many noble qualities, but under the cloud of adversity and the shock of disappointment it often fades away.

Not so the love of God! Let us look, for a moment, at what God Himself tells us of His love for His people. For one thing He does not tell us when it first began. His love is co-extensive with Himself. It was there, deep down in His own Being, from all eternity. It is therefore from everlasting to everlasting. Paul speaks of it in its four-dimensional nature —in its height, depth, length and breadth. It is like a vast sea without a shore to measure its breadth, and whose tide is always full. Its depths are unfathomable, and those who are borne away on its tide shall at last be brought to the blissful height of Heaven.

God also continued to love His people after they had ceased to love Him. Our Fall and our sin involved us all in scandal and shame. We fell into a state of rebellion and enmity against God. He created us perfect, but voluntarily and with our eyes open, we turned our back upon Him and said, 'Depart from us; for we desire not the knowledge of thy ways.' We had ceased to love Him, but His love continued as it was. We divorced Him from our lives but He refused to leave us. In justice He could have disowned us for ever, but instead of this happening, new and glorious disclosures of His love began to reach us, along with the promise of One who should come to rescue us from our state of peril. God loved us, then, not merely as He saw us perfect in our first creation, or as He saw us perfect in His Son. It was when we were defiled and slain by our sin that He entered our world to save us.

The love of God is, therefore, sovereign. He loved us, not for what we are but in spite of what we are and of what we did. As man now is, there is nothing in all that he is or in all that he does that could procure this great favour. Instead, everything repels. Our hearts within and our walk without are abhorrent to God's pure eyes. For God sees us not as we see ourselves; and what pleases us does not in this instance please Him.

To account for His love we must, therefore, turn our eyes from ourselves to that which lay in the depths of His own Being before the world was. This is what the Bible calls 'the good pleasure of His will'. It was this living stream moving towards man that gave exercise to all His attributes in man's salvation. This was the constraining power which moved Him to put the whole plan of redemption into operation. Behind what 'He purposed in Himself' to do, lay 'the good pleasure of His will'. This is the vast sea from which every stream of covenant favour proceeds. This is what lies behind all His gifts. As we stand, then, on this shore and view this uncharted deep we can only bow our heads and bless Him.

When, therefore, we ask the question why God loved us, all is wrapped up in silence. He loved us because He loved us: and beyond this point we cannot and dare not go. And so God Himself does not tell us when He began to love us —or why.

Love, of course, sees with its own eyes. Let me use an illustration. In one of our Hebridean isles there was once a young man who fell in love with a girl. He was tall, fair and handsome; but the girl of his heart was, in face and figure, plain and unattractive. When a friend asked him how he could possibly think of marrying such a girl he just smiled and said, 'O! If you could but see her with my eyes!'

And so Christ saw His Bride with His own eyes. But why He loved her is a mystery that shall sweetly engage her heart for ever and ever.

3

"The Sun is All Mine"

A Characteristic of God's love for His people is that it is both collective and personal. He loves them all equally and He loves them all personally. It embraces 'a great multitude which no man can number'. These are out of every race and belong to every generation. And He loves each as He loves all.

Modern science has in these days given us an awe-inspiring insight into the immensities of space and, to use a Biblical illustration, the incalculable number of stars which form the known universe. But man's mind is utterly incapable of expressing, even in mathematical form, the number of stars which come under our limited observation. And we have touched only the fringe of this vast unknown. It is all too big for our feeble comprehension. Only God knows the number of the stars. We have named only a few of these heavenly bodies; but, as the Psalmist tells us, He has a name for each and every one of them —'He tells the number of the stars; He calls them all by their names'.

In *Genesis* we read of how, on a quiet and cloudless night, God made Abraham look toward the sky with its vast host of stars. 'So shall thy seed be', the Lord said. That night God gave him a promise that not only would his natural seed be as numerous as the sand which is by the seashore, but that his spiritual seed —the children of light— would be numberless as the stars of heaven. For within that great utterance, 'In thy seed shall all the nations of the earth be blessed', there was also the promise that all these would derive their life and glory from Christ who is 'the bright and morning star'. For, as the stars receive their beauty and light from the sun, so the great multitude whom God loved shall for ever derive their life and glory from Christ, the 'Sun of Righteousness'. In heaven there is only one Sun —'The Lamb is the light thereof'. In that heavenly world those whom God loved in Christ shall shine as the brightness of the firmament and as the stars for ever and ever. Christ's Bride, then, in all her members, is not made up of a small company, but in their number passes far beyond the reckoning of angels and men.

Although God's love rests equally and permanently on such an inconceivable number it is not a mere general love lacking in those intimate and personal qualities which belong to the closer and more tender ties of life. God's love is, in fact, intensely personal. 'God loves each one of us', says Augustine, 'as if there were only one of us to love'. And this is how it is apprehended by all true Christians in their experience and in their enjoyment of it. This is how it is spoken of everywhere in the Bible; and the Christian consciousness bears witness to its personal quality. His love is personal, for He is a personal God. For example, God speaks of Abraham as His friend. Between Abraham and God there was a deep heart-to-heart communion. That communion was not wrapped in silence: they talked together as friends.

David also was constantly aware of God's presence and of His personal love in his life —'The Lord is my shepherd'. In his dying hour the pillow on which he rested his soul was God's personal relationship with him in Christ —'He hath made with me an everlasting covenant, ordered in all things, and sure'. And within this unbreakable tie his soul and body were everlastingly bound to God. Paul too could say in the light of God's promise and at the bar of his own wonderful experience —'The Son of God loved me and gave Himself for me'. The Christian woman who once exclaimed, 'I have Christ in my heart, I have Christ in His promise, and I have Christ in Heaven', gave voice to what we know of this personal nature of God's love.

A man sat one day in a garden. It was a warm day in summer, and the flowers, which were in full bloom, danced in a gentle wind. Resting quietly in his chair he remarked: 'How wonderful to be here! And the sun is all mine!' He did not mean, of course, that he had exclusive possession of all the natural blessings which streamed from the great day star. He knew that many millions of others could quite properly say the same. And yet his words were correct and appropriate, for the whole sun with its life, warmth and light was truly his. So might every Christian also say of Christ, the 'Sun of Righteousness', "He is all mine: His love is in my heart, His life is in my soul, His light is in my mind. He who is the Light of the heavenly world dwells also in my heart by faith".

The story is told of a young Christian man who once crossed one of those bays which are such an attractive feature of our Scottish west coast. He was alone. The bay was broad, but a kindly wind filled his sail so that he arrived at the other side without mishap. On being asked by a friend how it fared with him across the stretch of sea he quietly answered, 'The wind favoured me, and the Lord was with me'. 'I know', replied his friend, 'that the wind favoured you, but how can you tell that God was with you?' The impressive answer was: 'No one ever had Him but found Him warm in his heart'. Christ, in other words, had become the sun of his soul. He had the presence and love of a personal Redeemer in his heart —and he knew it.

A golden-haired little girl once lived in a Ross-shire parish. This girl had a problem which she could not solve: 'How can Jesus be in our heart and also in Heaven?' An older friend tried to solve her difficulty by pointing to the sun in the sky. If we turn our eyes to the sun, a little sun may be seen in our own eyes too. So when by faith we look to Jesus, the 'bright and morning Star', a perfect image of Him is begotten in our hearts. There is only one sun in the sky; but a true image of it may be seen in millions of eyes at the same time —if they just look towards it. And the little sun which is in the eye of the beholder is as real as the big sun which is up there in the sky! The Christ, in other words, who is in Heaven is the Christ who dwells in our hearts by faith.

These are only figures which may help us to see that, while God and His love belong to all His people, He is entirely and forever, and in a very real sense, the personal possession of each one. He is married to each one within the tie of a personal covenant. 'My Beloved is mine, and I am His'. This is the universal testimony of Christian experience.

4

Someone is Speaking

In the Godhead there are three Persons but only, as Augustine puts it, *una mens*, or the one mind. Therefore there is in the Godhead but one love. Although, however, God's love for his people is one and personal, the Scriptures speak of its several activities and manifestations as these are ascribed to each Person. We speak, for example, of the electing love of the Father, the redeeming love of the Son, and the sanctifying love of the Spirit. These, however, are but living streams flowing from the one great deep. The pearl of God's love —to change the figure— is something which we may admire in the light of revelation in its infinite beauty and variety. But as the Persons in the Godhead are equal, this love in its depth and duration has the same changeless quality also.

The Bible, however, speaks of the love of Christ —the second Person in the Godhead— for his people as having a peculiar wonder all its own. We say this although we really cannot tell which is the greater wonder —God giving us His Son or the Son giving us Himself. All we can say is that in the death of Christ for sinful men God's love is seen at its deepest and highest point. When the Scriptures say that Christ loved the Church and gave Himself for her we see His love touching a height beyond which it can never go. At that point its mystery deepens beyond all knowledge. It is, indeed, 'the love of Christ, which passes knowledge.'

Following this thought let us look for a moment into the eternal world through one of those brightly-lit windows which God has opened for us in His Own Word. As we look we may also listen, for Someone is speaking. "The Lord possessed me in the beginning of his way, before his works of old. I was set up from everlasting, from the beginning, or ever the earth was . . . Then I was by him, as one brought up with him, and I was daily his delight, rejoicing always before him, rejoicing in the habitable part of the earth: and my delights were with the sons of men." The Person who is speaking is called 'the Wisdom of God', or Jesus Christ, and He tells us that from all eternity His place of repose and rejoicing was in the bosom of the Father.

People who are perfectly happy at home have no desire to dwell elsewhere. And it may be said of Christ that He was infinitely happy in His heavenly home where He not only enjoyed the love of the other Persons, but also the love and adoration of the angelic hosts who surrounded His throne. Yet in the words quoted He speaks of His joy at the prospect of entering our fallen world—the world which was to be the scene of His humiliation, sorrow and death. He longed, in other words, for the day when He should inhabit our world and dwell among us. He was happy in Heaven; and yet those compassionate and love-filled eyes were ever looking beyond the confines of the heavenly world toward our mist-covered and fallen world where His loved ones were held in the unyielding grasp of sin and death.

The story of Jacob's love for Rachel is one of the great idylls of literature. The cruel conditions laid down by her father before she could become Jacob's wife involved a long duration of time and hard pitiless service. And, as time went on, his fond love-dream became shrouded in the dark folds of pain and deception. At the outset he knew but little of those privations and sufferings which lay across the hidden path of the future and which he had to endure before Rachel became his. At Bethel God had blessed him. There He had also promised him His guidance and His presence all his days. But a loving God left a mantle of concealment over his twenty years of tribulation in Padan-aram where 'in the day the drought consumed me, and the frost by night; and my sleep departed from mine eyes'.

God indeed is kind in hiding from us the trials which belong to the future. If the scroll of our personal providence were unrolled, even for a moment, before our eyes we could not endure the sight! In this concealment we see God's care for us and His infinite sympathy with our finite and enfeebled nature.

17

One of my boyhood memories is that of listening to a man over whose hearth Death had cast its shadow several times. In a broken voice he told his friend that if he had known beforehand how Death was to empty his home of his loved ones it would have been too great a sorrow to bear. God did not disclose to him beforehand the desolation and loneliness of his latter days. Instead, He was present Himself in each bereavement with the needed strength to enable him to bear it.

With Christ, however, there could be no concealment of all that He must suffer before He could have his loved ones with Him in the heavenly home. He is God, and as such, all things are 'naked and opened' before His eyes. He who is the Alpha and the Omega of all knowledge and of all events is the omniscient God. From the pinnacle of eternity He could see beforehand all the humiliations, the agonies and the death which He must suffer before His loved ones could be redeemed. He could see the manger where they laid Him, and the well at which He sat wearied with His journey through our world. He could see Gethsemane and Pilate's hall. He could see the awful cross shrouded in darkness and utter dereliction. He could anticipate that dread hour when, abandoned by God, He cried, 'My God, my God, why hast thou forsaken me?' He could see His own rejection and crucifixion by a nation whom He would have gathered under His wings. He could see the grave where He must lie for a season in the stillness of death. All this, and much much more, stood out before His all-seeing eyes. Besides, it was all written of Him 'in the volume of the book' —a book which He knew from cover to cover. And yet, as we said, those eyes, warm with undying love, were ever looking beyond those dread depths into which He must descend to the day when He would present His people to Himself in the world of Glory. "Who for the joy that was set before Him endured the cross, despising the shame: He shall see the travail of his soul, and shall be satisfied." "Christ loved the Church and gave Himself for her that He might present her to Himself a glorious Church." "For as the bridegroom rejoices over the bride, so shall thy God rejoice over you."

We have noticed already in our story that when Abraham wished to secure a bride for his son he made use of a servant. And Isaac himself expressed no desire to go into the far country to seek and win the one whom God had chosen for him. It may be that the ancient code of marriage etiquette demanded this initial aloofness. Or could it be that Abraham, as a fond father, was extremely solicitous of his son's welfare and safety? The long journey was fraught with peril and the distant desert was the haunt of ferocious beasts. Besides, evil men might lay hands on him. His only true son, the very apple of his eye, must not on any account be exposed to such dangers. The thought of his son going into that far country would have filled him with fear.

Now God in his Word describes our world as a far country. Because of sin it is alienated from Him and inconceivably distant from Him. It is sin alone that has created the awesome chasm between us and God. For all we know the rest of the creation is untouched by evil and may therefore be very near to God. Physical distance means nothing to Him. The real and infinite distance between Him and us is moral and spiritual. Our world is fallen; therefore it is a place of peril. Here 'wild beasts' in the shape of men and devils constantly prowl and destroy. God saw that, if He sent His Son into our world to redeem it, He would fare ill at our hands. Many would seek to tear Him in pieces. Indeed, the very people He loved and came to save would in their ignorance show themselves to be His enemies also. He was to be wounded and slain in the house of His friends! But God sent Him: 'God spared not His Own Son, but delivered Him up for us all'. And the Son wanted to come.

And as our Lord, so to speak, steps out of the eternal world into ours, He is faced with the deepest crisis through which He and our world ever passed. It was a crisis which His death alone could meet: 'Lo, I come to do thy will, O God.' Had He not come and had He not died we and all men would have sunk into the despair and darkness of a lost eternity. The chasm between us and God would have remained unbridged for ever. There would have been no marriage, and we would have remained eternally separate from God.

5

What the Elder Wrote

The very speculative, and indeed unscriptural, view has sometimes been put forward that since Christ is God He could have saved us without going through the appalling agonies of His life and death in this world. They argue that, because 'with God nothing is impossible', He could have redeemed and restored us in a way less distressful and less costly to Himself. Could He not have saved us by His perfect example, by His incomparable teachings, by His all-prevailing intercession, or by some exertion of His divine power? Is it not wrong, they say, to set limits to what God might have done?

The inescapable necessity, however, which lay behind the death of Christ we may discover in the first pages of the Bible. When the first man stood before God in the fullness of personal perfection God dealt with him as a moral and reasonable being. This, along with the precarious gift of an endless existence, was the dignity conferred upon him by his Maker. Man is, indeed, 'fearfully and wonderfully made'. And in the centre of the lovely garden where the first man and the first woman spent their holy and happy lives God placed a tree. It was the symbol of His loving and holy will, and it was meant to remind them always that their happiness lay in the path of a willing and loving obedience to God's Word. Man knew that as it was God's prerogative to command, it was his glory and privilege to obey. Truly this command was not grievous. It was neither arbitrary nor harsh. It was full of propriety and sweet reasonableness. God, indeed, could not have prescribed easier conditions of life. And as a mother warns her child, God had warned Adam and Eve against touching the only tree, out of a great many, which He claimed as His own. This was the kind and easy rule which governed their lives. It did not involve them in any toil or deprivation.

God, of course, knew that Evil was already present in the universe; but, as we have said, He had endowed man with knowledge along with ample power to resist it, should it ever assail him. And when it did assail him, man fell, against his knowledge and with open eyes. At that moment he lost communion with God. This separation necessarily involved him in death. As a flower cannot thrive once it is cut off from its own congenial environment, so it was with man. From the moment he wilfully cut himself off from God, he faded hopelessly into a state of decay and death. Not only so, but the penalty pronounced against sin was at once executed: 'The wages of sin is death'. 'Thou shalt surely die.'

Now when God, in warning man against yielding to evil, spoke of death He did not mean mere physical death. Nor did He mean that man in sinning would cease to exist. When God breathed His own breath into man's nostrils He in fact conferred upon him an immortal existence. That is how we can never cease to be. 'To be or not to be' is not therefore something left to our determination. The death which God meant was not only physical, but spiritual and eternal. Evil angels and men exist in a state of eternal but conscious death. In the sleepless torments of that state there is an eternal awareness of 'what might have been' if they had obeyed and loved the One they had cast aside. And since Adam was the federal or representative head of the human race the guilt in which he became involved in his first transgression is ours too. Besides, the poison which Satan, the old serpent, injected into his being is transmitted to us all. Because the fountain was tainted at the very source, the stream flowing from it is unwholesome and unclean. All mere men, therefore, enter the world ruined by sin and under sentence of death. They are born in sin and shaped in iniquity. They receive, in other words, the wages which they earned.

The question which now confronts us is, How could God redeem a race for Himself out of a fallen humanity? What means could his personal and unchanging love devise to secure restoration for his banished? How could He erect a new, pure and living temple out of this sad ruin? How could He be just in justifying and restoring those who, in effect, had said to Him 'Depart from us; for we desire not the knowledge of thy ways?' How could the ends of His justice and the unyielding demands of His law be met except through the execution of the sentence which He had pronounced against them? For He could not go back on His Word.

And God could not now accept satisfaction, in a matter which involved His infinite glory, from any person lower than Himself. The dishonour which sin had cast upon His glory was so great that He could accept no ransom from anyone who was not in every respect like Himself. And the one who would engage Him in this matter must be also a sinless man outwith the category of our fallen race. Man had sinned, and in justice man must die. Besides this, sin had already mastered all men and many angels. It had shown itself to be such a power as that only God, in the whole range of His omnipotence, could overcome and destroy. No angel however exalted could deal with it.

Now the universe could not provide such a one as this —one who, in order to satisfy God and to save man, must necessarily be God and man in one person. This was the mystery, or 'the problem', which no creature in Heaven or on earth could ever solve. It was something immeasurably beyond the wisdom and the grasp of the highest angels. Satan also might have concluded that, since God had cast him and all his followers into the place of despair, mankind in a similar state of rebellion against God must also share in that eternal doom.

It was at this juncture that God brought to light the way which His marvellous wisdom and grace had planned, whereby He could save man without any prejudice to His glory. The first hint of this hidden mystery reached our fallen world after He had, in the language of judgement, questioned Adam and Eve. The serpent which had deceived the woman was told that of the woman's seed One should come who would bruise its head. These words predicted the coming into the world of Someone who would vanquish Satan, destroy his works, and set free the people whom God had loved.

'The seed of the woman.' What did this mean? This is the first ray of light upon the deep, dark chasm between us and God, and which has brightened through successive ages. As the light of Revelation began to stream into the Church through God's Word, this first dim prediction became more and more astonishing in its sheer wonder. It meant that God himself was coming to save us. God was to become man that He might die for our sins. He was to take all our sins upon Himself and bear them away to an unknown place. God, in the Person of the Son, was to make an atonement for sin that He might reconcile us to God. This was 'the great mystery of godliness' which no finite mind could ever reach. It was, indeed, something infinitely beyond the apprehension of any creature. Christ, who loved His Bride, was to give Himself for her.

Coming into this mysterious, representative and substitutionary relationship with her He must, as justice required, die for her sin. Since He took her sin He must die her death. This was a fundamental demand of God's justice. But death had no legitimate claim upon Him. He died, therefore, voluntarily and in love. And the sweet engaging paradox implicit in what was, at the same time, a voluntary and a necessary death, is one of the hallmarks of His love.

A famous Scottish minister, Mr John MacRae of Greenock and Lewis, once brought this truth, of the necessity which lay behind the death of Christ, before his hearers in memorable words. He spoke of the Father as asking the Son if in loving His Bride He was still willing to rescue her out of that ocean of wrath where she was sinking. And when the Son had indicated His desire and longing to save His loved one, the Father said, 'If it be so, you must swim towards her in a sea of blood'. It was in other words through sufferings unknown, and through the shedding of His own precious blood, that He was to save her from the wrath and death which she deserved.

At the beginning of the Bible we read the story of how the first man obtained his bride without enduring any sufferings for her. God, we are told, put him to sleep. And as he slept, God transformed the rib which He took out of his side into the loveliest woman who ever walked on this earth. As God performed this miracle, the man, in deep and utter unconsciousness, might have been dreaming pleasantly of the broad rivers and the stately trees of Paradise. There was no sensation of pain. There was no disfigurement of his body; and no scar was left to show where the finger of God had touched him. When the man awoke out of that sleep he saw Eve, in all her sinless loveliness, at his side. It cost him nothing that she should be his.

It was not so, however, with Christ, the second Man from Heaven. When God took His Bride, in her very existence and life, out of His side He was fully conscious of all the spiritual and physical anguish which He had to endure for her sake. He was 'smitten of God, and afflicted'. Nailed to the Cross He could say: 'They pierced my hands and feet. I may tell all my bones: they look and stare upon me'. (Ps. 22) As in her stead He drank the cup of woe which He found in her hand, He refused that other drink which was meant to dull His consciousness and lessen His pain.

The following story, so rich in pathos and meaning, was once told by a preacher to his congregation. A young man had called on him that he might attend the funeral of a loved one who had died giving birth to a child. "When I saw her dying", this young man remarked, "I would willingly have given myself over to death for her sake. But this I could not do." These words bring before us human love in its noblest form, but also in its helplessness and despair. Death is cruel. He is our enemy. He is unmoved by our tears and deaf to our cry. In his hand we expire; for we have no power over him. And Christ saw His Church expiring in the relentless grasp of death. He knew that the price of her salvation was that He should die for her. Only by His death could death be slain and made to give up its prey. This was what His love constrained Him to do. The minister mentioned was so deeply moved by the depth of affection which lay in the young man's heart for the one in whose stead he could not die, that he used the story to portray the deeper love which moved the Son of God to lay down His life for His people.

Paul's firm assurance of this wonderful fact is embodied in his words, 'The Son of God, who loved me, and gave Himself for me'. Every saved sinner may stand before the Cross of Calvary, and also re-echo his words. They remind us of the man who once expressed in broken English the ground of his hope for Eternity: 'He no die, me die. He die, me no die'.

It is this fact of Christ coming into our world to save us by His death, and thereby to enrich and unite us to Himself, that makes the gospel the Good News. "For ye know the grace of our Lord Jesus Christ, that though he was rich, yet for your sakes He became poor, that ye through His poverty might be rich." It is, indeed, good news that those who enter the world under sentence of death and deep in debt to God should have that sentence remitted and the debt removed. It was by His perfect obedience and perfect sacrifice that He discharged to God as our surety all the heavy debts we had incurred, and which we could never hope to repay. For if we could not pay the first farthing of this incalculable sum how could we hope to pay the last? This heavy indictment He nailed to the tree, blotting out the handwriting of ordinances which was written against us. Therefore it is written: "Who shall lay anything to the charge of God's elect?   . . . It is Christ that died . . . " God's law is at peace with us. His Justice threatens us no more with eternal imprisonment for the debt we owe. God in all His attributes smiles upon us. Before the Cross, 'Truth and Mercy meet: Righteousness and Peace kiss each other'. Heaven and Earth are there reconciled.

In the *Epistle to the Hebrews* we are told that long before Christ entered our world and long before He died He made His last will and testament. And all that He had He left to His Bride. But this testament could have no validity and its riches could not be administered till He died. 'For where a testament, is, there must also of necessity be the death of the testator'. It was His death that purchased for her an inheritance of eternal glory and felicity in heaven. His riches are unsearchable and beyond all calculation, He had enough to pay for her debt, and much more to spare. All the spiritual riches of His grace and glory are willed over to her in all their fullness. It is in this act of paying her debts that the Bride sees His infinite love for her soul.

There lived once in the North of Scotland a worthy man of God who was an elder of a Church. He was also a merchant. In his day poverty was not unknown in the land. There were those to whom he had given credit, but who found it difficult to repay him. Now he was on his death-bed. Knowing that his last hour on earth was near, he asked a member of his family that he might have the book which detailed all the debts that his poor but honest neighbours owed him, but, which in the stress of poverty, they could not hope to pay. As he turned over page after page he wrote 'Paid' across each one till he came to the end. This was truly an act of grace and kindness.

And so when Christ bowed His head on the Cross and cried 'It is finished', He meant that He had paid for ever to the Law and the Justice of God all that had stood out against His people. He had, in other words, written 'Paid' over the record of that debt which they could never hope to pay. This truly is good news for all who know that they have nothing to pay for what they owe to God. It is good news also that, as He died to pay her debts, His life ensures that nothing of what He left her shall pass her by.

We once knew a Christian woman whose husband had died in a foreign land. He was a man of means and he had intended that his wife and children should inherit a competent share of his wealth. But his riches went through so many hands and such lengthy processes that a relatively small portion of his inheritance reached her. But Christ's Bride is not left on the lap of uncertainty and insecurity. Her riches and treasures are beyond the grasp of any dishonest hand. There are many who would deprive her of her spiritual inheritance, and because Her husband is 'He that lives, and was dead' she shall enjoy the whole. For if it were saved by His death, 'much more, we shall be saved by His life'. He lives to put into our possession without fail what His death has procured. His inheritance and riches are therefore 'sure' to all who love Him. "I give unto them eternal life; and they shall never perish, neither shall any man pluck them out of my hand."

Before we could live, therefore, Christ must die. Before we could enter His Kingdom He must first enter His world.

There are also other things which must happen within the context of our personal lives and experience before we can enter into His Kingdom. But this is the theme of the next two chapters.

6

The Man in the Garden

On a summer morning, in a seaside village in Wester Ross, an old man who was also a choice Christian suddenly stood still and began to listen. At that moment the sun was pouring its first beams of soft light over the distant Cuillin hills. The early morning boat from the Western Isles had arrived, and was now lying in the stillness of the morning at the pier. And someone was singing a Psalm. It was the most appropriate song that could be sung at that hour. The voice was rich and musical, so that in the deep calm of the dawn it carried far across the bay. The words sung were from Psalm Nineteen, which speaks to all of God's glory as it may be seen in His creation.

The heavens God's glory do declare,
The skies His hand-works preach:
Day utters speech to day, and night
To night doth knowledge teach. . . .

In them He set the sun a tent;
Who, bridegroom-like, forth goes
From's chamber, as a strong man doth
To run his race rejoice.

As the old man listened, he was deeply moved not only by the quality of the voice, but by the deeper significance of the words which reached his ear. 'The Bridegroom'; 'The Sunrise'. Did he not remember Another whose name is the 'Sun of Righteousness', the 'bright and morning star', and whose 'goings forth have been from of old'? He remembered how He had left the chambers of the heavenly world that He might run His race 'down here' and finish with joy the work which His Father had given Him to do. It was He who arose with healing in His wings on our fallen sin-sick world, and Who in a storm of suffering and death sank into the grave, but who arose again on the third day in the power of an endless life.

The promise that Christ, the light of the world, and the Redeemer of His people, should appear in the fullness of time engaged His people's prayers and interest in every generation. As Christ rejoiced in the prospect of coming to redeem His own, the wistful eyes of the Bride were ever turned toward the heavenly world, waiting for the promised day when He should come over the mountains of time and separation. "Until the day break, and the shadows flee away, turn, my beloved, and be thou like a roe or a young hart upon the mountains of Bether." The Psalmist also gives voice to the same thought and longing: "My soul waits for the Lord more than they that watch for the morning".

Sometimes those who wish to enjoy a clearer and more impressive view of the sunrise climb a mountain that they might, with its rising, feast their eyes on the colours and the glories of the sky. In the same way the Bride, during the whole of the first dispensation, speaks of herself as on the mountain of myrrh, and on the hill of frankincense waiting, in prayer and patience, for the dawn of day when her Lord should appear. And He came as was predicted of Him in His Word and in answer to her prayers.

But here we are confronted with man's deepest tragedy. It is the tragedy of his total spiritual blindness. When, for example, in the physical world we are unable to see the sun our blindness is complete. And not to see the glory of the Lord in His Person, Word and Ministry is the appalling proof that we are not only in darkness, but that we ourselves are darkness. The extent of our 'religious' light, our intellectual and moral attainments, fail to relieve this state of man; for if 'the light that is in thee be darkness, how great is that darkness'. This is what sin has done. The God of this world has blinded our eyes. This was why, when He who is the brightness of God's glory appeared in this world, multitudes passed Him by. They saw no beauty in Him that they should desire Him: 'The light shined in darkness; and the darkness comprehended it not'. This is how we all are until, by a miracle of grace, the veil is removed from our eyes.

There is a famous picture entitled 'The Blind Girl' which has a deep spiritual meaning. In that picture the sky is replete with beauty. A double rainbow spans the heavens, while in the distance the sun is breaking through a cloud. The earth below, with its vivid pastoral touches, is ideally lovely. But the blind girl sees nothing. She lives in a world of perpetual night. Her companion, whose eyes are full of light, is enraptured at the scene, but she can convey nothing of what she sees to her friend. And if she tried to do this, her blind friend would not understand.

The picture could be a parable. There is another world and a glorious Saviour, whose loveliness we shall never see till our eyes are opened. Those in whose lives God had wrought this miracle of enlightenment could say when Christ appeared in the world, 'We beheld His glory, the glory as of the only begotten of the Father, full of grace and truth'. This, too, was the subject of Paul's prayers on behalf of his Ephesian converts. "That the Father of glory may give you the spirit of wisdom and revelation in the knowledge of Him: the eyes of your understanding being enlightened, that ye may know what is the hope of his calling . . . And to know the love of Christ which passes knowledge." And without this unveiling of our inner eyes by the power of God's Spirit we shall never see the beauty of Christ. This should be the subject of our prayers, for He came to give the blind their sight.

These remarks remind me of a brief talk I once had with a stranger in the Glasgow Botanic Gardens. It was summer. The day was bright and warm. The flowers and the trees which feast the eyes of those weary city dwellers who love to relax there for a while were full of beauty and life. This stranger who shared my seat that afternoon was anxious to talk. And the subject of his remarks was what he called 'true religion'. Like many of his kind he advanced the view that if we did our best, if we lived 'the good life' and loved our neighbour, then surely God would give us a place in heaven at last.

After a moment of silence I asked him a few apparently irrelevant questions. 'Do you see the sun up there in the sky?' 'Of course I see it', he answered. 'And you see these flowers which grow in this garden, and the people who walk about?' 'Yes, I do', he replied, eyeing me somewhat strangely. 'And do you know why we see these things? Is it not because we are here and that we have the precious gift of sight? Actually, we see these things because we were born into this lower world of nature. If we had not been born we would see nothing. We would in fact have no existence at all.'

I then drew his attention to an incident recorded in the Gospel about a learned Jew who once interviewed Jesus Christ. This very religious and cultured man wanted very much to know who Jesus was, and how He did those miracles which were such a remarkable feature of His public ministry. He wanted to know something about His kingdom and His divine power. However, instead of giving a reasoned explanation of His Person, and of 'the world' to which He and His followers belonged, our Lord simply said: 'Ye must be born again'. In other words, Christ would have him realise that with all his 'goodness' and 'religion', he could never hope to know anything about Himself, or His power, or of His heavenly kingdom unless he was first born into that world of spiritual reality and grace to which the Lord and His people belonged. It was not enough that he be born within the circle of a church and a member of a favoured people. Heaven required another birth and a higher relationship.

It requires, in other words, a spiritual birth to know spiritual things. Just as any knowledge of the natural world presupposes our birth and normal powers of perception so without this miracle of grace we just cannot know Christ or see His kingdom. I never saw my friend again, but I hope he took to heart the meaning of our Lord's words, that the Church in Heaven is, by a deep inescapable necessity, designated the 'Church of the first-born'.

There is another thing that requires to be said at this point. Those who imagine —as so many do— that they could enjoy heaven without this new nature have to reckon with the terrible fact that, since their sinful nature is hostile to God and to everything which is of God, they could not endure Heaven for one half-hour. And Heaven could not endure them. Such would far rather be elsewhere than in Heaven. No creature can survive in an environment which is hostile and uncongenial to its nature. It would be easier for a man to survive in 'a consuming fire' than for an unconverted sinner to endure the eternal weight of glory, holiness and love which shall be the spiritual and blissful environment of the redeemed in Heaven for ever.

We have, for example, known those on earth to whom God's Word, God's people and God's house were utterly repugnant. And yet some of those people think that they could enjoy an everlasting fellowship with God and His people in Heaven. This is as impossible as it is irrational and unscriptural. It is not going to happen. 'You *must* be born again'.

It was this spiritual rebirth that endowed with spiritual insight and recognition those who beheld the hidden glory of the Lord while He was here on earth. 'Who were born not of blood, nor of the flesh, nor of the will of man, but of God.'

It was not, therefore, the literary and prophetic beauty of the Psalm, or the quality of the voice, which so much moved the emotions of that man of God as he listened on that early morning to the Psalm. It was his apprehension of Christ's loveliness and of His great love in leaving the chambers of Heaven to redeem His people, and His returning thither again with the salvation of all His people secured. He could also thank God that all this had been revealed to him by the Holy Spirit, and that by God's grace he was to participate in that glory which shall be revealed in all those who love His appearing. Both Scriptures and experience prove, then, that in a state of sin we have no spiritual perception.

The Scriptures also predicted that Christ, the Heavenly Bridegroom, would, for wise and just reasons, enter our world in disguise. He would appear not only in the garments of absolute holiness but also in the garments of poverty, humiliation and suffering. It was necessary that He should enter this world without visible glory or outward splendour. If he had appeared otherwise the world could not have endured the sight of His infinite majesty. In coming as He did, we see His loving condescension and His sympathy with our fallen state. He appeared in the likeness of sinful flesh. His face was more marred than any other, and His form more than the sons of men. He came as a man of sorrows —bowed down under the weight of our sins which God had laid upon His heart.

And when He did come He entered our world unobtrusively. Few knew that He who lay in the bosom of a woman, unable to walk and unable to speak, was the Creator and Sustainer of all things. He humbled Himself and 'took upon Him the form of a servant'. For thirty years of His earthly life He dwelt in obscurity. Some members of His own family, even, were unaware of the solemn fact that He who shared their pillow and their table was the eternal God in man's nature.

Those who were looking for a Messianic Prince of earthly power could not reconcile the lowly Man of Nazareth with their own wishful thinking—which had no basis in the prophetic Word of God. They were looking for one whose kingdom was to be of this world and who should go forth to subdue all nations. Although the scriptural and spiritual 'signs' of His Messianic character were present in His life and in His works and words, they rejected Him. They had no eyes to see that, covered by those garments, He was their God. This homeless Person whose very followers were drawn from among those who had no social distinction or ecclesiastical status could not surely be 'the Star of Jacob' or the King of Israel! Thus there was no recognition of His glory and therefore no acceptance of His claims. 'There stands one among you whom ye know not.' Only His Bride, born from above and enlightened by the Holy Spirit, knew His voice and recognised His face.

It is this spiritual recognition and acceptance of His Divine glory and claims that brings unending joy to all His people. But how sad to think that He is still, in the life of many, the unknown and unwanted Redeemer of men. Let me illustrate this fact by the following story.

Many years ago a quaint-looking minister preached in the Church of St. Nicholas in Aberdeen. His appearance was so odd that an amused smile could be seen on many faces in the large congregation that came to hear him. But as the service continued the smiles vanished and instead many were moved to tears as they listened to his words. In the life of many present it was a memorable hour. God's power had touched many hearts. Hundreds were asking the old but all-important question, 'What must we do to be saved?' The strange minister went on to quote the words: "Behold I stand at the door and knock; if any man hear My voice, and open the door, I will come in to him and will sup with him, and he with Me". He then pictured the Lord of glory, patiently and lovingly, standing at the door of men's hearts and waiting to be welcomed and received, but still unknown and unrecognised.

In the course of his sermon he told a story of a young Scottish prince of a bygone age who, in disguise, knocked on the door of a nobleman's palace. It was the day when his only daughter was about to celebrate her coming of age. Many suitors were waiting for her hand. Leaning on a crutch and dressed as a tramp, this disguised prince asked if he might see the young lady who was being honoured that day. When at last she came to the door she asked him of his errand. 'I have come', he answered, 'to ask your hand in marriage'. For a moment she looked into his face and then put out her hand and said — 'Very well. Here it is'. The tramp, with evident joy, then asked about the day when the marriage should take place. The young lady replied, 'This day twelve months hence'. The incident was much enjoyed by her attendants who were looking on, and who thought it a good and easy way of getting rid of such a poor, unbalanced wretch. But the incident ceased to be amusing when, on that day and throughout the intervening months, she refused every offer of marriage on the grounds that she had already given her heart and hand to another. Her father pleaded with her not to act so foolishly as to tie her life to an unknown pauper. But nothing

34

would move her from her purpose. She had given her word and made her choice.

It was exactly a year from that day that the inmates of the castle heard the sounds of many pipes and drums. And over the crest of a distant hill they saw a procession moving toward them, headed by the king's son riding his favourite steed. He was no longer the unrecognised 'tramp' in rags, for he came dressed in royal garments. He had come as he said he would, and at that castle door his loved one stood waiting for him. It was then that the astonished company realised who the disguised and ill-clad visitor of the year before really was. She alone had recognised him then, and in recognising him she had pledged herself to be his forever.

The minister who told this story was the famous Lachlan MacKenzie of Lochcarron. The story was meant to warn his hearers against judging by appearances. The Lord of glory entered our world in disguise. We little know who Christ Crucified is. Many exclude Him from their lives. The offence of His Cross is still a persistent obstacle in the way of many. For Him there is 'no room in the inn'. We welcome others, but Him we leave to stand outside. He is still standing at many a door, unknown and unwanted. But what anguish awaits all those who refuse Him when, surrounded by the hosts of the heavenly world, He shall re-appear in all the dignity of His exalted glory. 'I was a stranger and ye took me not in' is a fearful judgement to face. And only those who had recognised and welcomed Him when He knocked at the door shall be admitted into His glorious presence to share in the fullness of joy which is for ever more at His right hand. (Ps. 16)

Our salvation, therefore, required not only that He should love and redeem us. It requires also that by a miracle of grace our souls should be quickened, and our inner eyes unveiled, and that all barriers between us and God should be removed.

7

The Barriers Dissolved

Christ came into the world, then, not only to redeem His Bride but also to enlighten her eyes from His own glory and worth, and to win her to Himself by His Word and Spirit. But there are other suitors on the scene who would claim her heart and hand.

Although there is no hint of this in the story, it would be difficult to conceive that a young woman of Rebecca's appearance and known qualities of mind and disposition would have no suitors in the land of her birth. We cannot tell. We know, however, that when Jesus Christ confronts the sinner with His plea, 'Give me your heart', other suitors are present to oppose Him and to snatch, if possible, the precious soul out of His hands.

It is a fact that the opposition to God's call is both real and terrible. It can also be subtle and deceptive. These other suitors often dazzle our eyes with the false but coveted prizes for which so many strive; but they hide the fact that all who listen to their voice choose the path of despair. Christ Himself was tempted by Satan. He was presented with a view and an offer of all the kingdoms of this world and their glory. The only condition was that He should renounce His purpose of doing His Father's will. The same temptation, in a thousand different forms, is presented to men and women in every age. But the dreadful mirage has no basis in reality. It is wrapped up in a lie. It leads to the precipice of utter spiritual destruction.

Those who oppose Christ and would claim our heart and life, are known in the Bible as a trinity of evil. They are often spoken of as 'the world, the flesh and the devil'. These are they who strive for man's soul. Those who listen to their voices and submit to their conditions can never again find the path of life. But the last word is not with them, but with God and with the sinner himself.

Once Mr Rowland Till addressed a large crowd in the open air in one of our English cities. As he pleaded with the people to choose Christ and life, rather than sin and death, a magnificent carriage appeared at the scene. Inside was an attractive bejewelled young lady who was that evening to dine in the palace. The driver demanded a right of way through the crowd, but the earnest, if eccentric, herald of God cried, "No! Before you pass I offer this lady for sale. Already there are three bidders on the scene but it is left to her to say which of these is her choice." This incident and its happy sequel are perpetuated in verses which preserve the words of the preacher and the wonderful conversion of Lady Anne Erskine, the lady of our story.

'Twas in the king's broad highway,
    Near a century ago,
That a preacher stood -though of noble blood -
    Telling the fallen and low
Of a Saviour's love and a Home above,
    And a peace that they all might know.

All crowded round to listen;
    They wept at the wondrous love,
That could wash their sin and welcome them in
    His spotless mansion above:
While slow through the crowd, a lady proud,
    Her gilded chariot drove.

'Make room', cried the haughty outrider,
    'You are closing the king's highway:
My lady is late, and their Majesties wait;
    The preacher heard and his soul was stirred,
And he cried to the rider, 'Nay,
    'Tis the king's highway, but I hold it today –
In the name of the King of kings."
    Then bending his gaze on the lady,

And marking her soft eye fall—
'And now in His name, a sale I proclaim
    And bids for this fair lady call,
Who will purchase the whole - her body and soul,
    Coronet, jewels and all?

'I see already three bidders —
    THE WORLD steps up as the first:
'I will give her my treasures, and all the pleasures
    For which my votaries thirst;
She shall dance each day more joyous and gay,
    With a quiet grave at the worst.'

'But out speaks THE DEVIL, boldly:
    'The kingdoms of earth are mine,
Fair lady, thy name, with envied fame,
    On their brightest tablets shall shine';
His eye like the lightning flashes,
    His voice like a trumpet rings—
'Only give me thy soul, and I give thee the whole,
    Their glory and wealth, to be thine.'

'And pray, what hast thou to offer,
    Thou MAN OF SORROWS unknown?
And He gently says: 'My blood I have shed
    To purchase her for mine own;
To conquer the grave, and her soul to save,
    I suffered the cross alone.
Your grand fete days, your fashions and ways,
    Are all but perishing things.

'I will give her my cross of suffering,
    My cup of sorrow to share;
But with endless love, in my Home above,
    All shall be righted there:
She shall walk in light, in a robe of white,

And a radiant crown shall wear.'
'Thou hast heard the terms, fair lady,
    That each has offered for thee.
Which wilt thou choose, and which wilt thou lose,
    This life or the life to be?

She took from her hands the jewels,
    The coronet from her brow;
'Lord Jesus', she said, as she bowed her head,
    'The highest Bidder art Thou;
Thou gav'st for my sake, Thy life, and I take
    Thine offer —and take it now.'

'Amen', said the noble preacher;
    And the people wept aloud.
Years have rolled on—and they all have gone
    Who formed that awestruck crowd,
Lady and throng have been swept along,
    On the wind like a morning cloud.'

But Saviour has claimed His purchase;
    And around His radiant seat,
A mightier throng, in an endless song,
    The wondrous story repeat;
And a form more fair is bending there,
    Laying her crown at His feet.

Did Lady Ann Erskine meet Bethuel's daughter Rebecca in heaven? All who are there have a story to tell. It is the story of how the Lord loved them, drew them to Himself with 'cords of love', and enabled them to make Him their own for ever.

A few years ago there died in this country a Christian lady who, when a girl, had a remarkable dream. In her dream she saw herself playing with a number of companions. As they were playing a glorious Person stood among them who asked each one what she particularly desired in life. With eager eyes and words each expressed her wish. Some wanted lovely homes. Others wanted money and material comforts. Others wanted gaiety and pleasure. But when He asked the girl of our story to state her desire she simply said, 'Take my soul with Thee to Heaven to live'. This was the only answer which seemed to make the Lord rejoice; for as He looked into this girl's face He smiled and said 'It surely shall be done'. She smiled too; for she felt that her prayer was granted.

And the remarkable thing was that the dream of May Shayler of Oxford —for that was her name— came true. By a strange process of Providence she lived to see the companions of her night thoughts each possessing the earthly gifts wished for, while she herself was led by the Spirit of God to choose the 'good part' and the 'one thing needful', and for the remainder of her life to devote herself entirely to the Lord and His cause. And here we are confronted with the terrible fact that we sometimes get what we desire — like Esau who chose a perishing blessing rather than eternal life. Only those who embrace Christ have a lasting treasure in Heaven. The rest move toward eternal impoverishment.

The opposition to Rebecca's call came from another, and perhaps a more dangerous, quarter. It came from those who loved her dearly within the tender ties of nature. It took, as we mentioned, the form of procrastination. Her people in Haran would have her stay for 'at least ten days'. Certainly she would go later, but not at once. Was this a mere sentimental reluctance on their part to say a final farewell to a much-loved daughter and sister or was there another reason? Conceivably it might have been that before God's messenger appeared on the scene something had been arranged which required her presence, and that the messenger's demand for her immediate departure clashed with it. It could be. All we know is that the ensnaring shadow of delay fell on her path. And although Rebecca, to her eternal gain, did not do so, this is how many tamper with their destiny.

We have heard of some whose hearts had been deeply touched by a Gospel appeal. In the recesses of their spirit a voice seemed to plead with them to make an instant break with their sinful ways and to come to Christ at once. But for reasons of their own, 'tomorrow' seemed more suitable than 'today'. And so they carried on. Gradually the inner voice ceased to trouble them. By delay and excuses they let the time of their visitation pass till that warning voice was silenced, and the candle of spiritual opportunity had gone out for ever. Their death-bed prayers met with a closed door and a remote and silent God. Satan can ensnare us through our earthly friends and cherished pleasures. Many find that his 'ten days', so desirable at the time, culminate in forfeiting eternal life.

There are not only voices and influences from the world outside that would oppose our coming to Christ, but there is also that within ourselves which works in opposition to God. Sin, in whatever way it may show itself, is a barrier between us and Christ. The sin barrier in our own hearts may assume many forms. It may take the form of prejudice, guilt, ignorance, pride, a conscious aversion to God and the Gospel, or the fatal 'excuse'.

In His parable of the marriage of the King's Son our Lord speaks of that great event as being associated with God's loving-kindness toward men. In the fullness of His mercy He furnishes His table and sends forth His servants to welcome all who will to the marriage supper of His son. And surely no one would decline the incomparable honour and privilege of participating in this feast of eternal joy in communion with God and His people.

But what should have been an occasion for joy became an occasion for sorrow. God's messengers who had gone forth with the good tidings returned in due time sad at heart and deeply apprehensive of the fearful retribution which would overtake those who made light of His goodness. Those to whom, in the first instance, this good news came were so preoccupied with the inferior claims of this present world that they could not give God's call any serious thought. Some were courteous and respectful in their refusal. Otherwise violent and resentful.

These looked upon God's call as something which encroached on the only 'world' they desired to possess. Excuses began to multiply. These were Satan's stepping-stones into the place of Despair. They were his masterpieces of distraction and deception. The farmer whose mind was earth-bound; the man who preferred the beasts of the field to God and eternal life; and the one whose marriage had involved him in some form of religious neutrality or compromise, could not come. At the bar of their own reasoning such excuses were, no doubt, perfectly valid and reasonable, but at the bar of God's judgement they were not so. They merely intensified their guilt.

Unbelief is another of the great barriers between us and Christ. In the final analysis, the 'good news' contained in the Gospel comes to us from the very heart of God —the God for whom it is impossible to lie. But opposite these 'glad tidings' of great joy we place a question mark and adopt the fatal attitude of doubting. We do not, in reality, believe the 'good news' at all.

When the Queen of Sheba heard the story of Solomon's riches and renown she at first dismissed the matter as a mere 'tall story'. Nothing could have removed that barrier of doubt from her mind apart from her very wise decision to go and see for herself. And her faith led her out of her doubt till the full truth of what she had heard passed into her own experience. 'It was a true report that I heard in mine own land . . . Howbeit I believed not the words, until I came, and mine eyes had seen it; and, behold, the half was not told me.'

Now Rebecca's decision was entirely based on faith. She had never seen that wealthy prince who lived in the distant land of Hebron. The sincere servant whom she encountered at the well might have exaggerated the story of his master's dignity and wealth. And supposing the story should be true, would she command his interest and affection if she agreed to go? And why did this young prince not come himself instead of sending this man? Besides, her going away demanded her separation from her home and her people. And were there not hazards in the way? Yes, Rebecca could have raised a thousand questions such as these, but her faith triumphed over them all. It leaped over every chasm of doubt and unbelief. She believed that the story was true; and that somehow her eternal destiny and safety were involved in her decision. There were many questions to which she would have liked an answer; but meantime the first step —'I will go'—must be taken in compliance with God's call. And that first step was to be followed by an ever-growing light upon her path and an ever-growing realisation of God's faithfulness and truth.

How often have we listened to and read of the more wonderful story of God's love for sinners. It has probably reached our ears and eyes hundreds of times. Every time we listen to it we either 'do not care', or perhaps we ask ourselves a series of questions. Is it true? Is there really such a place as Heaven? Does Christ really love sinful men and women? Is it not too much to believe that He does come into such a relationship with poor mortal creatures? Can I believe those men who preach the Gospel and who tell me that God has sent them to plead with me to accept Christ and His gift of eternal life? Is it worthwhile to forsake a 'real' world for a world which may not exist? 'The story is wonderful, no doubt, but. . . .'

And so it is written that many could not 'enter in because of unbelief'.

But whatever form the sin barrier between us and Christ may take, it can be removed and destroyed. God's saving power is greater than the power of evil. His power can pull down the strongholds of sin within our hearts and enable us to overcome all opposition and temptation from without. The power of the Holy Spirit is irresistible and can, therefore, break through all barriers of evil within and without the soul of man. "For the Word of God is quick, and powerful . . . piercing even to the dividing asunder of soul and spirit." The Gospel of Christ when accompanied by the Spirit 'is the power of God unto salvation to every one that believeth'.

This deliverance from sin's dominion coincides with an instantaneous passing out of one state into another or with our

43

spiritual translation out of the kingdom of darkness into God's marvellous light. And when the barrier between us and God is dissolved we become aware of His new life within us.

The break-through of this divine power can be experienced in many ways; but whatever the experience that may precede or follow it, the event itself is instantaneous and final. Many, like Paul, could speak of the explosive moment when, overwhelmed by surprise, they stood face to face with God. The old world was shattered and gone and they found themselves standing on the threshold of another. They could also speak of that unutterably sweet moment when, instead of a sense of guilt and fear, the love and peace of God took possession of their hearts. They could tell of the real conviction that they were now living in a new world. All things had become new. They no longer looked through Christless eyes at God's wonderful creation, or at the universe around them. Every flower and every star seemed to smile upon them. This is what entered into the experience of the Bride as she tells us in song: "My beloved spoke, and said to me, Rise up, my love, my fair one, and come away. For lo, the winter is past, the rain is over and gone; the flowers appear on the earth, the time of the singing of birds is come . . . " We also have known those who had felt the dark shadow which had rested on their spirits giving way to the first tokens of a new spiritual summer. A woman was once questioned about her spiritual qualifications for admission to the Lord's Table. She said that she knew God had given her a new heart for she was now living in a new world. It was the time of her first love.

This marks the birth of the soul. Our sky clears, for death and darkness are swallowed up in life and light. When by faith we see God's glory 'in the face of Jesus Christ', and taste of His love, all resistance is forever at an end. It is then that we sing a new song.

He put a new song in my mouth,
    Our God to magnify:
Many shall see it, and shall fear,
    And on the Lord rely.

Just as I am —Thy love unknown
   Has broken every barrier down —
Now to be Thine, yea, Thine alone,
   O Lamb of God, I come.

In this act of grace and power God does not force our will. He knocks that we may open. He draws that we may come. We are made willing in a day of His power. He gains the Bride's consent to be His, not by any arbitrary compulsion, but by drawing her with the bands of His love. But at what point the sovereign power of God begins and the will of man ceases to rebel we cannot know. We do know, however, that at the moment when, by God's enabling grace, our fingers touch the latch of the door to welcome the Blessed One into our heart, heaven is begun.

There are, of course, many genuine believers who cannot speak of the ecstatic moment when Christ passed by them and said 'Live', and when His love and forgiveness first became real. Their experience lacks this initial assurance —this sudden dawn after a long starless night. But a sense of need, daily bringing us to Christ, is as valid a proof of being in a state of grace as our spiritual enjoyments and vivid experiences —however precious these may be. Let me illustrate this as follows.

One day two eminent scholars met in the city of Edinburgh. Both were humble Christian men. The one asked the other as to his spiritual welfare. "I am poor indeed", was the reply. "I am aware of three evils in my heart. There is a sense of guilt in my conscience, of rebellion in my will, and of darkness in my mind." And then he made the comment, "I can say, however, that I would welcome into my poor soul Christ as my Priest to take my guilt away, as my King to subdue me to Himself and as my Prophet to enlighten my mind in His own knowledge".

What a deep insight we have in these words into the nature of true faith in Christ who in his fullness stands opposite the needs and the evils which lie within our hearts. The three chief rooms, as it were, which make up our real selves we would have Him to occupy for ever. In this way He dwells in our heart by faith.

'Nature', we are told, 'abhors a vacuum', and for the soul of man there is nothing more dangerous than 'the empty house', however well it may be garnished and swept. Our souls are made to be occupied, and in the ultimate sense they can be occupied only by either God or evil.

Man, as God created him, cannot endure the loneliness or emptiness of an unoccupied life. To throw away by a mere negative effort at self-reformation 'our dearest idols' without a worthwhile replacement only paves the way for even greater despair. Our Lord reminds us in one of His parables that the latter end of such is worse than the first. The devil is deceptive; for although he may leave us alone for a season he will, without fail, return to his old haunt to leave us no more. God grant that Christ and not 'the strong man armed' may dwell in our hearts.

Once I met a woman who was in a state of great anxiety. She had been a Roman Catholic, and for reasons of her own she was led to renounce the false tenets of the papal system, but as yet she had found nothing to put in their place. She had cast away a false religion, but had not yet found the true.

As I told her of Christ who is the Pearl of great price, and the One who could give her living water and everlasting peace, she listened wistfully to my words. From that day —as I have reason to believe— God, in taking possession of her heart, gave her a new song and blessed her with His own unsearchable riches.

Faith is therefore a receiving grace which is born in the soul through a sense of need. All to whom the Spirit of God has revealed their sin and need turn from themselves to embrace this great salvation which is in Christ alone. Such bring nothing in their hands. The need is theirs. The fullness is His. These are they who are His guests at His table and who have His promise "If any man hear my voice, and open the door, I will come in to him, and will sup with him, and he with me." When the door of our heart opens, the last barrier is gone. Christ is our Guest, and we also sit at His table for ever.

8

The Banquet and What Some of the Guests had to Say

As a rule, every marriage has its banquet. There is that hour of good will when all who assemble bestow their best wishes and their smiles on those who now stand in a new and life-long relationship to one another.

Now the Heavenly Marriage also has its feast. The Bride in the *Song* says, 'He brought me to the banqueting house'. This is the feast that God had prepared for His guests before the world was.

When we look forward to welcoming to our homes our dearest friends, we begin to prepare for their coming before they arrive. The season of happy fellowship we anticipate warmly. And so God, before He called any of His people to His marriage supper, had His table furnished, and the blessings set in order for His guests. Nothing is lacking of what we need or what we desire. 'My God shall supply all your need according to His riches in glory by Christ Jesus.' When we come into a state of grace, and when we enter the upper world of glory He welcomes us in these words, 'Come, for all things are now ready'. These spiritual blessings are stored up for us in Christ. Our salvation here and our glory afterwards are enjoyed and reserved in Him.

The joys and blessings of this feast are not therefore something unknown, remote and reserved in Heaven. In a state of grace we get our daily portion here of what we hope to enjoy in a fuller measure by and by. The Bride is spoken of as having 'honey and milk under her tongue'. These were the choice blessings of Canaan; and yet while still journeying through the desert she is refreshed and sustained by Heaven's nourishment. The love of Christ, which is sweeter than honey, is in her heart; and the 'sincere milk of the word' is the secret of her strength. The prophet Isaiah speaks of God's feast as consisting of 'fat things full of marrow; of wines on the lees well refined'. Among men, the more ancient the vintage, the better the quality and the sweeter the flavour. But what shall we say of that love which is 'better than wine' and which was not only in God from everlasting, but which comes to us 'well refined' through the sufferings and death of our Lord. The language of true Christian experience is always the same. 'The Lord is the portion of my soul.' 'O taste and see that the Lord is good.' There is an assurance of God's love, peace of conscience, joy in the Holy Ghost, and a constant supply of grace till we reach the end of life's road.

Those who have tried to express in words the joy associated with God's feast have found themselves almost embarrassed and silenced. It is 'joy unspeakable and full of glory.' They know, as by instinct, that it is something which belongs to another world, and which impoverished nature here could not bestow. True believers who enjoy, in some measure, the love and presence of Christ in their heart know how wonderful such an enjoyment is. We knew of some who wished for death rather than lose that inconceivably blissful 'something' which sometimes, and quite unlooked-for, had entered their soul and left them amazed that they could experience such a depth of happiness.

If Heaven is this state of bliss made constant and unending, no wonder though the Holy Spirit should use words the meaning of which we cannot now comprehend. "For since the beginning of the world men have not heard, nor perceived by the ear, neither hath the eye seen, O God, beside thee, what he hath prepared for him that waits for him." (*Is.* 64)

With such 'tastes' of God's love there is also an apprehension of the glory of Him from whose fullness such enjoyments come. When Jonathan tasted of the honey which lay in the wood his eyes cleared and his vision returned. With life comes light. With the enjoyment of God comes an insight into His glory. Taste, and then see. Rebecca, for example, not only enjoyed tokens of her husband's riches, but her ears were also charmed by the story of his dignity and greatness. And in the Gospel those who received out of Christ's fullness, and 'grace for grace', were those who also beheld His glory, 'as of the only begotten of the Father, full of grace and truth'.

The three supreme notes of the Everlasting Gospel are— Who Christ is, what Christ did, and what Christ gives. He is infinitely glorious. He died to save us. And He gives Himself as our eternal portion. This is the message God blesses in winning souls. As Abraham's servant made his master's dignity, kindness and wealth his only theme, the theme of every true herald of God is the glory of Christ, His great love in dying for us and the spiritual blessings which He is willing to bestow on all who come to Him.

The Bride herself ever dwells on the loveliness of her Lord. It is her voice we also hear on the last page of the Bible. 'The Spirit and the Bride say, Come . . .' Everywhere she informs us that to taste of His feast brings with it a disclosure of His own surpassing glory, and that His life is the light of men.

Such insights and enjoyments as we here mention belong to a very real world. Those who live in conscious communion with God are, in fact, much nearer to reality than those who exist on the circumference of life, distracted and deceived by the Enemy whose aim is to keep them in that state of impoverishment and estrangement from God for ever. No serious student of the Christian life, from whatever angle he deals with the subject, can deny that spiritual love, joy and peace in God are aspects of ultimate reality deeper and more solid than anything belonging to this present world. But as the Christian life can only be understood from 'the inside', we cannot hope to convince those who are 'outside' that its satisfactions are such as we describe. Only those who are guests at Christ's table know how good is the banquet. And no one who ever sat at this feast would exchange it for another; for here we have all that the heart can desire —and much more.

In terms of strict reason the outsider is, in fact, incapable of judging the true quality and nature of the Christian life. It is a life of which he knows nothing. It is a world which is spiritually beyond his reach and knowledge. To the mere 'natural man' its claims are not only unintelligible but 'foolishness'. But the foolishness is all on his side.

On the other hand, a true believer in the Lord is able to make a just comparison between the old life and the new. He knows both worlds. He has lived in and to some extent has explored both. His judgement should, therefore, command our respect, if not our acceptance. The younger son of Christ's parable, for example, could make a just evaluation of the old life and the new. We know that once he had tasted of the feast with which his father had celebrated his home-coming he no longer desired to go back to the pigs, the prostitutes and the dunghill of his old degenerate days. But who would accept his 'views' of the Christian life while he still lived a spiritual bankrupt in the 'far country'? And yet how often have we heard of men and women without any spiritual existence, or Christian perception or experience, passing judgment on God's feast, as if they had tasted every dish on His table!

Right down through its long history the Church of Christ has been blessed with men and women whose voice on this subject we ought to hear. In many instances these were people of material wealth, of incomparable intellectual gifts and of the highest culture and the brightest earthly prospects. Some of these were also of the highest moral and 'religious' attainments. They had been offered and given the best which this world could provide. But it was only when they had tasted of God's love and salvation that they realised how emaciated were their souls, and how empty the 'cisterns' from which they had tried to satisfy the spiritual void within their hearts. And, if we refuse to hear such, it simply means that deep irrational prejudices fester within our minds which close them against all reasonable conviction.

In the life of Moses, for example, we are confronted with a man whose stature, opportunities and background are perhaps the most colourful and impressive in history. He knew both worlds intimately. He knew the world of human grandeur at its best, and he knew the better life of personal devotion to God. There was a moment in his life when he was asked to choose between these two. And he chose to serve God in preference to all the riches, honours and pleasures of an earthly kingdom. This he did, not when he was an unthinking youth, or an old man whose mental powers were in decline. He did not decide in an hour of 'overt emotionalism' which modern psychology insists is necessary for religious experience. He was not motivated by frustration. He was not an unfulfilled man who had tried and failed. He stood at the height of his powers, with his foot only two steps from the throne. He could have indulged all his natural desires. By one word he could have inherited the vast riches of a great kingdom. Nothing was withheld from him. But his answer was decisive, final and irrevocable. "By faith Moses, when he was come to years, refused to be called the son of Pharaoh's daughter; choosing rather to suffer affliction with the people of God, than to enjoy the pleasures of sin for a season; esteeming the reproach of Christ greater riches than the treasures in Egypt: for he had respect unto the recompense of the reward."

Moses did this because he had a deep spiritual appreciation of that other world, the blessings of which are abiding and whose riches, honours and rewards are everlasting and unfading. By faith he saw another King and another country. He tasted of the inconceivable joy of communion with God. Therefore he bade an everlasting farewell to the inferior offers of this mortal life. He chose to serve Christ's Bride in her garments of suffering and to become her son, rather than enjoy the easy indulgent smile of Pharaoh's daughter —with all the transient gifts and comforts of this world.

Many years after his departure from Egypt, and years of suffering in 'the great and terrible wilderness', he met a friend to whom he offered the rich and enduring rewards reserved for those who truly follow God. "We are journeying unto the place of which the Lord said, I will give it to you: come thou with us, and we will do thee good: for the Lord hath spoken good concerning Israel." These words show that he never once looked back. There was never any regret on his part for his choice. For that reason he died with the word 'happy' on his lips. He went to Heaven along the road of self-denial, and bearing the Cross of his Lord.

History provides us with an even more impressive story of disillusionment and discovery. It is the story of a famous king. This man's wealth had passed all the limits of calculation. His reign coincided with a period of great political tranquillity. His sky was without a cloud. He had access to every form of pleasure. On his shoulders rested every honour and royal dignity which this world could confer. God had also endowed him with special wisdom and rare aptitudes of mind. Nothing escaped his observation, and his proverbial philosophy reflects a penetrating and comprehensive survey of the total sum and value of 'all things under the sun'. But the more he searched, the deeper his disillusionment became. He discovered that, in all that he had and saw, there was nothing that could give him spiritual repose and inner happiness. All was 'vanity and vexation of spirit.' This was the cry of despair of the wealthiest and wisest of men. All creation was impoverished. There was no feast here for the soul of man. Like Augustine he had discovered that only God could rest and satisfy the heart which He had created for Himself. But God changed his dirge of despair into a superlative song. The day he found Christ his soul emerged out of its shroud into a state of joy and inner peace. 'I sat down under His shadow with great delight, and His fruit was sweet to my taste.' This was the *Song of Songs* of King Solomon after he had tasted of God's feast and had seen the loveliness of the Son of God.

God has so ordered it that in every age men should give their testimony in favour of the infinite superiority of God's grace to every other blessing. Are not Augustine, Pascal, Calvin, John Howe, Madame Guyon and C. S. Lewis —to mention but a few— incomparable intellectual and spiritual persons who have reported well of God's good land, the fruit of which imparts eternal life to those who believe?

I know that some of these testimonies reach us over the void of many centuries. They belong to the more 'primitive' ages before science had evolved the many social and domestic 'comforts' of our times. But our age of material welfare is also the sin-sick age of violence and despair. The age of technical 'progress' and knowledge is become the age of fear and discontent. Modern man needs God, as did those men of other days. Indeed, the so-called modern man of today will be the ancient man of tomorrow. Fundamentally, he is the same in every age —a sinner in need of God.

Not many years ago, for example, a famous doctor closed his door in Harley Street in London and went out into the great world of humanity to preach the 'good news' which had so richly blessed his own life. He had discovered that the Gospel, and not a progressive and highly valued medical science, held the secret of spiritual healing and eternal life. His colleagues looked upon him as a rising star in the medical world. When someone expressed his surprise that he should give up the bright prospects which lay before him he said, 'By following Christ and becoming a preacher I have gained everything and lost nothing'. This man had discovered that Christ and His Gospel are the answer to our deeper spiritual needs, and to the perilous trends of the world of today.

On a different level is the story which I am now reading of a young woman who had danced her way towards the floodlights in the world of entertainment. The cheap honours and empty applause of the world she served dazzled her eyes. But the farther she travelled along that garish, noisy road the deeper became her despair. The cry of her empty heart reached the ear of God, who came and blessed her with forgiveness md peace. It was when she received this gift of eternal life that she realised that what had eluded her all her days was, by faith in Christ, now settled in her heart.

This then is the voice and witness of all true Christians. Those who are 'inside' know. The rest don't. This is the universal testimony of all who have tasted that the Lord is gracious. His guests never go elsewhere. They never want to leave His Home. And they never shall.

Who with abundance of good things
Doth satisfy thy mouth,
So that even as the eagle's age
Renewed is thy youth.

9

"Home, Sweet Home"

If a man who had lived all his days in obscurity and poverty were asked to dine with royalty, he would, no doubt, consider himself as very highly honoured. The day would at last arrive when respectful and courteous servants would usher him into the royal presence. He would touch her hand, enjoy her smile and hear her voice. At her table he would sit down for a while. But in that palace he cannot stay. The hour would arrive when he must bid her good-bye and depart. In that kind and courteous way laid down by court etiquette he would find himself at last passing through the palace gates, never to enter them again. He is outside. The great occasion is over. Now he sits in his own humble home with only a fading recollection of that day and of the privilege he enjoyed.

But in the kingdom of grace it is not so. As God's children we not only sit at His table, but we stay in His Home. Born and adopted into the family of God we have a right to all the privileges of His sons and daughters. God is now our Father in Christ and we enter His Palace to go out no more. He who is our portion is also our eternal Home.

Poets down the ages have been weaving a golden halo around the word 'home'. When Rebecca ended her journey and entered her home she must have felt that sense of wistful enjoyment which, they say, is in the heart of every bride as she stands on the threshold of her own home. But the pleasing sentiments which are associated with the words do not altogether fit the widespread domestic tragedies of this age. For many the words, 'Home, sweet home' have only the embittered ring of disillusionment. For others, whose homes are blessed with harmony or, better still, the felt presence and peace of God, home, indeed, is 'sweet'. It may be a place of unhappiness, or a place of rest and quiet enjoyment.

The tragedy of man as a fallen being is that while he may have his uncertain home here, where his mortal self may momentarily dwell, something tells him that he is spiritually homeless and a wanderer under the sun. Like the dove that went out of the ark he flits to and fro, never finding rest. Is there not in his heart also a nostalgic pain which goes to prove that once upon a time he was happy in God? The great saying of Augustine is true to all human experience. 'Thou hast made us for Thyself, and our hearts are restless till they rest in Thee.' There is much truth in the words of the poet:

This is not a place for thee;
Never doubt it, thou hast come
By some dark catastrophe
Far, far from home.

It was this sense of spiritual estrangement that welled up in the soul of the younger son of Christ's parable when he found himself longing for the home which, in his folly, he had left. He was not driven out of that home. He left it. So it is with man. 'Left to the freedom of his own will' he parted with God. But throughout the great waste over which he wandered he has found no rest.

Man without God is indeed like an orphaned child who frets for the bosom and love of his mother. We may try to calm and distract his little mind and instincts with unsatisfying fare and alien sounds or empty toys, but unconsciously he yearns for the lost joy of her breast, the sight of her face, the touch of her hand, and the sound of her sweet, endearing voice. In other words the soul of man can rest only in God. Our Lord tells us of a man who tried to quieten his spirit with 'much goods laid up for many years'. But he failed to still his restless, apprehensive spirit. This was the man whom God called a 'fool'. Mere things can never give us peace. The fatal flaw at heart of a Godless materialism is that it seeks to fill the vacuum in man's soul with the promise of an earthly paradise into which God must not enter!

Long, long ago the words were written: "Lord, You have been our dwelling place in all generations. Before the mountains were brought forth, or ever You had formed the earth and the world, even from everlasting to everlasting You are God". These words tell us that long before the universe came into existence God had a place for men in His love and purposes of grace.

Why did Christ dwell among us here with nowhere to lay His head? Was it not that He might gather us to Himself? He was homeless that we who had none might have a home in Him. To all those who came within the reach of His glorious voice on earth He said: 'Come unto me . . . and I will give you rest'. And on earth when men passed Him by He wept over the eternal consequences of their refusal. How often would He have gathered them 'as a hen gathers her chickens under her wings'; but they would not. And here I want to tell a story which might serve to illustrate how true all this is in human experience.

In the days when it was a crime in England to preach the Gospel outwith the pale of the State Church, a young girl was the means of saving a godly servant of Christ from prison and banishment. She was only a child but, because of her kindly act of intercession on his behalf, the man concerned invoked upon her head the blessing of the Triune God for time and eternity. Then, forgetting his words, she went her way to spend her life and fortune in an empty round of amusement and gaiety. Wherever she went and whatever she enjoyed, her heart remained empty and her spirit restless.

One Saturday night in London she went to bed and dreamed. In her dream she saw herself on the way to an unknown church. She saw many people hurrying into this church. Following the eager throng she found herself sitting in a pew listening to the singing, the prayers and the sermon. It was all so real and so very wonderful. The minister took for his theme the words of Psalm one hundred and sixteen: 'Return unto thy rest, O my soul; for the Lord hath dealt bountifully with thee'. When she awoke the dream remained in her mind with startling clarity. She felt that in some mysterious way God and her destiny were present in her vision.

When she awoke on the Sabbath morning she told her companion that she felt she ought to go to church. London, as we know, is a vast city, but after much searching she was amazed to see the very people of her dream hurrying toward a certain church. It was the same building, and the service was exactly, word for word, as she had seen and heard in her dream. Her palpitating heart was deeply affected by the sermon, which was on the very words of that Psalm. It was all about the rest which is in God for the homeless soul of man. 'Sweet words these!', she thought within herself. And the mystic dream became a living reality. The forgotten prayer of God's servant was at last answered. God had remembered it, and at the set time He answered it in the conversion of her soul. Then for the first time she knew that the secret of peace and joy could be found only in God. She also knew that what she enjoyed of this peace on earth was a mere earnest of the perfect peace and rest awaiting her in Heaven with the Lord.

How beautifully is this sure hope of an 'eternal home' with God expressed in our Scottish Paraphrases and in Watts' famous hymn.

> O spread thy covering wings around
> Till all our wanderings cease,
> And at our Father's loved abode
> Our souls arrive in peace.
>
> O God our help in ages past
> Our hope in years to come
> Our shelter from the stormy blast,
> And our eternal Home!

As the Home is eternal so also is the bond of union between us and Christ. 'Because I live ye also shall live.' Earthly ties are necessarily dissolved, but 'who shall separate us from the love of Christ'?

Dr. Andrew Bonar once called on a Christian lady whose home had been desolated by death. As he approached this home of sorrow he wondered what appropriate word of sympathy he could leave with its lone inhabitant. But as the door opened these words, enframed on the wall, met his eye: 'They shall perish; but thou remainest'. Here it was: '*Thou* remainest'. Christ, in the unchangeableness of his promise, His love and His sympathy, is the solid foundation of all true comfort. The ray of sure hope which reaches us from this promise should brighten our darkest night and sweeten every cup of sorrow which God in His providence might apply to our lips.

A minister once told his congregation of an incident which was meant to strengthen the assurance of God's children, and which is a fit comment on how the Lord, who is forever with His people, is able to sustain them in every trial. It is the story of a young girl who had trusted her soul to Christ and to whom He had given a promise that, bound to her in covenant faithfulness, He would be her true Friend for ever. To this young woman her conversion was so astonishingly wonderful that she immediately bought a Bible, which became her greatest treasure in this world. God's statutes became her songs. But her upbringing and religion, which she had now renounced, brought her under severe persecution in her home. One day she had to flee with only her Bible in her hand. But one of her pursuers tore it out of her grasp —all but one leaf. When at last she reached a place of safety she looked at the torn but precious fragment in her hand. 'When my father and mother forsake me, then the Lord will take me up.' These were the words which fell as a balm on her spirit. Did this happen by a mere coincidence or chance? No. It was God Himself, who had so miraculously preserved these words, present in the promise and reminding her that she could not be separated from His love and care. 'This God is our God for ever and ever.'

10

Jewels for the Bride

God has provided not only a home and a banquet for His people, but also precious spiritual jewels and raiment which adorn their persons, as they take their place within His palace. These not only cover and beautify them, but they also identify them as His chosen ones. In Psalm Forty-five we get a picture of Christ's Bride, the Church, adorned in these and entering the palace of the King where she is to meet her Lord face to face. And since Rebecca is a fit type of the believer, let us look at her again as she appears before us in our story, thus enriched and arrayed.

The gifts which Abraham's servant presented to Rebecca were meant to show that God's call was real and without deception. They were the visible tokens of an inheritance far greater and richer than anything Bethuel's household could conceive. The gifts were both costly and full of beauty; and they were given with a liberal hand as if they were but the smaller earnests of better things to come. As the precious gems were one by one brought forth, the household could only express themselves in words of delight and surprise. Their hearts must have been deeply touched at the high honour which had been conferred upon their child.

Most of the gifts were, of course, given to the bride. There were rings to adorn her fingers, along with bracelets and raiment. These all graced her person as she went forth, with her maids accompanying her in the way. As the cavalcade moved away, amid the farewells and benedictions of her people, she did not look back. Her heart was already with him who was waiting for her in the distant land beyond the 'mountains of separation'. As she journeyed thither through the land of her adoption her garments and jewels would proclaim who she was. By them she could be easily recognised as Isaac's bride.

The spiritual significance of all this is plain. When in a day of God's power we are made willing by the Holy Ghost to follow Christ, we are given tokens of His love and earnests of our inheritance. These are spiritual gifts and graces by which we are identified as His people. There are inward enjoyments and outward adornments. God's Spirit dwells in us, and the love of Christ is 'shed abroad in our hearts'. We are given great and precious promises which, like a treasure, we hide within our heart. The graces of the Spirit —faith, hope and love— are born within us when Christ, the hope of glory, is enthroned in our heart. Christ, the 'pearl of great price', enriches our soul for ever. These are spiritual jewels of which no one can ever deprive us.

In John Bunyan's immortal dream we read of Little Faith who, on his way to the Celestial City, was waylaid by thieves, who robbed him of the loose coins he carried on his person. But they could not find his jewels, which were hidden away in a secret place. Bunyan, by this allegory, means that God's people on their way to Heaven may lose many of their comforts, but they cannot lose Christ, who dwells in their hearts by faith. They may lose God's conscious presence and mourn for many days under a sense of spiritual desertion. They may lose the comfort of His Word, and a sense of His love. Their sun may hide itself, and their sky may for a season be without a star. Their jewels, however, are safe. He is unchangeable in His love, in His promise, and in that Covenant which is 'ordered in all things and sure'. Our life is hidden with Christ in God. Our real treasure is beyond the reach of the spoiler. The 'great goodness', earnests of which we enjoy here, is eternally secure beyond the reach of every enemy.

There is another spiritual 'jewel' which lends both honour and dignity to all who know the Lord. In our union with Christ we bear a new name, given to us by the Lord Himself. The new creature in Christ bears new and endearing names which testify to His love for us, to a new relationship, and to our place in His family. "Behold, what manner of love the Father hath bestowed upon us, that we should be called the sons of God." "Thou shalt no more be termed Forsaken; neither shall thy land be termed Desolate: but thou shalt be called Hephzibah, and thy land Beulah: for the Lord delights in thee."

Perhaps, indeed, in Rebecca's eyes the most esteemed gift was the comely robe which adorned her person. And there is no gift which Christ's Bride values more than 'the best robe' of His own glorious righteousness. In His righteousness she is accepted of God, justified in His sight, and exalted to God's right hand, both in her new relationship and prospects. This is the theme of her song. "I will greatly rejoice in the Lord, my soul shall be joyful in my God; for He hath clothed me with the garments of salvation, He hath covered me with the robe of righteousness, as a bridegroom decks himself with ornaments, and as a bride adorns herself with her jewels."

When Bunyan's Greatheart was on the road with Christiana he charmed her ears and warmed her heart by telling her of Christ's two coats —one of which He had no need of, and could therefore give to anyone who had none. In his excellent comments on this exalted theme he tells her that Christ has a righteousness which is essential to Himself as God but which He cannot give to any other. There is also the coat of His mediatorial righteousness which, as the God-Man, He wrought out by His life of perfect obedience to God in His law, and by His meritorious death on the Cross, and which is now available to His people.

Under the law the High Priest in Israel had, so to speak, two coats. These were the garments of glory and beauty which he habitually wore as he ministered before the Lord. There was also the 'holy linen coat' in which he ministered on the Day of Atonement in the Most Holy place. This great event took place once a year, when he sprinkled the blood of the Covenant before the mercy seat which lay between the cherubim. After performing this awe-inspiring service, the High Priest divested himself of this single holy garment, and was clothed again in his habitual garments of 'glory and beauty'.

Now Christ in a state of humiliation divested Himself of all visible glory. In His life and death He wore the 'holy linen coat' of spotless holiness which, we think, typified not only His humiliation but also His mediatorial righteousness which, as the God-Man in one Person, he wrought out for His Church. When on earth He finished the work in righteousness, He divested Himself of this 'holy linen garment' and returned to the Upper Sanctuary arrayed again in His habitual garments of beauty and glory which, as High Priest over the house of God, He shall wear for ever. But the linen coat is ours. He left it behind Him. In these typical figures there lies the profound and eternal truth of God's grace in imputing to all His people the spotless mediatorial righteousness of Christ, in which they stand for ever before Him 'without spot'. 'The Lord our righteousness' is the foundation of our eternal security and glory.

Even now we may hear part of the song which the saints sing in Heaven. "Let us be glad and rejoice, and give honour to Him: for the marriage of the Lamb is come, and His wife hath made herself ready. And to her was granted that she should be arrayed in fine linen, clean and white: for the fine linen is the righteousness of saints." 'She shall be brought unto the King in raiment of needlework.' The Apostle John, in his vision, saw 'a great wonder in Heaven, a woman clothed with the sun.' He who is the Sun of righteousness shall clothe her for ever. With Christ's imputed righteousness, which is fundamental to all her favours, there is also an imparted righteousness and a reflected righteousness. The one is a righteousness of nature which she receives in her regeneration. The other, in which she walks in newness of life and reflects the beauty of her Lord, marks her out as Christ's 'epistle' which may be 'read of all men'.

There was a lovely incident in the life of the Duchess of Gordon which she often mentioned. One night, in a state of spiritual anxiety, and as she lay sleepless, there appeared before her eyes a white scroll of unearthly brightness. Written at the head of this scroll in letters of gold were the words, 'The Lord our Righteousness'. All her darkness was dispelled in a moment, for she believed that Jesus was made of God unto her righteousness, and that His shed blood had made her whiter than snow. Her soul immediately entered into perfect rest, and she rejoiced in the full assurance that she had both righteousness and strength in the Lord.

The all-important question which now confronts every one of us is this. Have I renounced for ever my own righteousness that I might be clothed in His? True faith not only embraces Christ as our exclusive and perfect righteousness, but also involves a total and final rejection of all our personal 'goodness' as a ground of justification. The younger son in the parable was stripped of his rags before they clothed him in 'the best robe'. And all who sit down at the marriage feast in heaven must be clothed in the wedding robe provided, not by themselves, but by the King. None can enter His court in what their own hands have woven. A sordid covering of 'good works' may appear fair enough to many but it will never satisfy the requirements of God's Holy Law and of Heaven. The Apostle Paul prayed that he "might be found in Him not having his own righteousness, which is of the law, but in the righteousness which is of God by faith". And the Lord's people in every age pray that at the end of the day they may be found 'in Him' in that same way.

When Rebecca appeared before Isaac there was, on his part, instant recognition. His bride wore his own jewels and the garments which he had given her. In the same way when the Church of God, in the person of all believers, arrives at His door, He shall receive and welcome her into His palace. She comes adorned by His grace and righteousness. But the Word speaks to us of 'foolish' ones who substituted their own 'goodness' for His, and an outward formality for inward grace. When they knocked at the door there was no recognition. Instead they heard the solemn words, 'I know you not'. Too late they made a discovery of their utter folly and unpreparedness.

But Christ still dispenses His gifts with a liberal hand. His words to the proud but foolish Church at Laodicea apply to us also. "I counsel you to buy of me gold tried in the fire, that you may be rich; and white raiment, that you may be clothed, and that the shame of your nakedness do not appear." These priceless blessings we may buy 'without money and without price'.

When to His call and offer we say, 'I will go', in that moment God's Spirit opens the treasures of His grace, and provides us with the first solid tokens of the great inheritance awaiting us in a better world.

11

"The Bride Says, Come"

God provided such great and unfading blessings for us, and would therefore have us know about them. Christ's last command to His chosen apostles and to His ministers in every age is, 'Go ye into all the world, and preach the gospel to every creature.' The home is prepared. The table is set. Garments and jewels befitting the occasion are provided for all who come. The welcoming voices which reach us are from the very vestibule of glory. 'Come; for all things are now ready.' 'The Spirit and the bride say, Come, and let him that hears say, Come . . .'. 'Compel them to come in, that my house may be filled.' God's Holy Spirit who thus strives and pleads with men is He who makes God's call effectual to salvation. The free offer of the gospel is therefore a great evangelical treasure since it comes primarily from God, the Holy Spirit who, as He invites us, is able to make us obey His own voice. 'Come' is a favourite word with Christ. It should therefore be a favourite word with us. It is His Word we preach, and it has therefore the same authority on the lips of those whom He sends as on His own. It is a word which God has often and very richly blessed in the conversion of souls.

Let us, in imagination, sit for a moment at a service held in the heart of London many years ago. The famous Metropolitan Tabernacle is, as usual, packed with eager worshippers. During the service many are the tears in the eyes of those who listen to the famous preacher, as he pleads with them to come to God's gospel feast. Many hearts are melted down in penitence while new and strangely sweet emotions arise within their spirits. God's Spirit is truly present. The incomparable voice of the famous preacher rises and falls as he repeats the words: 'Compel them to come in, that my house may be filled.'

Spurgeon used to say that there was not a seat in the Tabernacle which the Holy Spirit, at one time or another, had passed by. But this particular sermon stands in a category all by itself. It marked a point where in that sacred building the tide of God's power had touched new heights. Many could trace the beginnings of a happy eternity with God to that great sermon. 'Compel them to come in: all things are now ready.' 'The marriage of the Lamb is come, and His wife hath made herself ready.' 'Come, come, come.' And from many hearts came the genuine but silent response: 'I will go.'

We have already mentioned the personal nature of God's love. His call and invitations are personal also. On earth our Lord often ignored the crowd, and addressed His words to some solitary soul who wanted healing from sin and its plagues. It was so with Zacchaeus and Bartimeus, with the woman at the well, and with her who touched the hem of His garment. The relationship between God and man is awesomely personal. In our ultimate moral and spiritual accountability to God we stand alone. Within the circle of destiny and judgment we stand apart and remote from all other men. Each of us must give an account of himself to God. Both in His judgment upon our lives and in His gracious dealings with us He brings us into isolation. This is what we also discover when God's call impresses itself savingly upon our spirit. 'He calls them all by name.'

When God's voice arrested Saul of Tarsus he was no longer one of the troop. 'Saul, Saul, why do you persecute me?' That voice isolated him and brought him into the searching light of God's presence. It was a voice of judgment and of grace. And how personal was his answer: 'Lord, what will You have me do?' He was alone with God.

An American traveller once found himself sitting in Spurgeon's Tabernacle. He was amazed at the vast, eager crowd who had come to hear a sermon. He wondered how one man could command the interest of such an overwhelming multitude. The waiting, excited crowd fascinated him. But when the service began he was entirely captivated by the wonderful voice and the evangelical fervour of the preacher. His mind was so held by the message that the crowd at last faded out, and he could see and hear only God's herald who proclaimed the 'good news' with such earnestness to the people. As the sermon proceeded he heard another voice. It was the voice of God, speaking to him in His Word. There he sat face to face with the awful realities of eternity, and as if no one existed within the universe but God and himself. It was a voice which drew his heart to the great Saviour whom Spurgeon proclaimed.

In the Highlands of Ross-shire there is a sheltered hollow near which flows a fern-kissed stream, known as 'the Burn of Ferintosh'. In this quiet and picturesque dell many people used to gather in other days to hear the gospel. One day the minister of the parish, the famous Doctor John Macdonald, left his manse with a great burden on his heart. He yearned for the salvation of the lost. When he stood up to give his final address of exhortation to the vast multitude who had assembled at the Burn he based his remarks on the words, 'Hearken O daughter, and consider, and incline thine ear.' (Ps. 45. 10) These words he dovetailed into the words of our story: 'Wilt thou go with this man?' As he went on pleading with the people to 'kiss the Son' and to yield to His claims and accept His overtures, the great congregation was deeply moved. Then from among the crowd a voice was heard. It was that of a tall, comely, middle-aged woman who cried, 'I will, I will, I will.' Many wept out of the depths of their hearts. This was not a passing wave of emotionalism, for many lived in later years to praise God that they were there on that day, when God's Spirit moved their hearts to embrace the Prince of Life. God honoured His Word and promise in the salvation of many. That message God's Spirit used in opening many hearts to receive the gift of life eternal.

Another spot in the Highlands, in Gairloch, Wester Ross, is famous for its evangelical associations. It is known as 'the White Cow's Bed'. This green circular hollow, with its ample accommodation for over two thousand people, used to be the scene of great religious gatherings. In that quiet hollow, men like Doctor John Kennedy of Dingwall used to preach the everlasting gospel in all its sweetness and power.

Many years after Doctor Kennedy and his faithful contemporaries were no longer on the scene a young minister was asked to preach in Gairloch. And those who heard his words could see how true he was to the Gospel note and emphasis of those old heralds of God. His name was John Macleod who afterwards became Principal of a theological college in Edinburgh. His sermon in Gairloch was on the one word, 'Come.' The centre of his theme was the welcome which God extended in His Word to sinners. Some who listened to his words that day were deeply touched as they recalled the days of old. The message was so true to the great Gospel tradition which had brought such blessings to the land. It assured those who were seeking salvation that Christ's heart is tender and full of pity toward those who are ignorant and out of the way.

A few years before he died this great scholar and theologian wrote a book. It was on the theology of the Reformed Church and on all the errors and distractions through which it had to survive throughout the years. In this book he deals with the manner in which both an extreme Calvinism and a shallow Arminianism had, in their presentation of the Gospel, lost the ideal balance between God's sovereignty and man's personal accountability to God. And since we are dealing with the Gospel call in this chapter we cannot do better than quote his words. We ought to take them to heart, for they show the solemn and inescapable relationship in which man stands to God as he is presented with the free offer of salvation in Christ.

"In regard to the claims of God, each of these extremes worked from a common principle which they turned to opposite ends. The Hyper-Calvinistic brethren held that there is no world-wide call to Christ sent out to all sinners to whom in the letter the Gospel comes, neither are all bidden to take Him as their Saviour. On the other hand, they maintained that Christ is held forth or offered as Saviour to those only whom God effectually calls. They reasoned that man, as a bankrupt in spiritual resources, cannot be called upon to do what is out of the compass of his power. He can neither repent nor believe.

So it was out of place to call upon him to do what he cannot do. In this, when we look into it, we find the common Arminian position that man's responsibility is limited by his ability. The Arminian holds to the presence of a certain ability in those that are called; otherwise sinners could not be called upon to repent and believe the Gospel. Each side takes up the principle from its own end. They fail together to recognise that the sinner is responsible for his spiritual impotence. It is the fruit of sin; and man's sin does not destroy nor put out of court God's right to ask for an obedience alike in service and repentance and faith that His sinful creatures have disabled themselves from yielding to Him. His title to make His demand is entirely and absolutely unimpaired. He claims but His own when He bids man, made in His likeness and for His glory, serve Him and be the doer of His will as He makes it known. When He calls upon him to repent He but asks what He is entitled to. When He bids the sinner who needs the Saviour receive Him as His own, He is altogether within His rights in doing so. There is a glorious superiority to man's reasonings shown by Him who bids the deaf to hear and the blind to look that they may see.

"The obligation to obey God holds, and this makes it our sin not to honour it. It is our sin that we do not repent when we are called upon so to do. It is equally our sin if we do not believe and obey the Gospel when it tells us of our Lord and bids us take Him as our own. This sin is the crowning sin and it decisively marks out the unbeliever as the enemy of Christ the Lord. Those who give place in their thinking to the defective and erroneous principle that there is nothing to answer for when there is no power to obey, can find no place in their teaching for commending the Gospel except to those who are already under Divine tuition and have learned to some purpose that they are lost sinners. So the open way that the Gospel sets before the sinner which he may take—and must take—in coming back to God is as good as shut when this type of preaching limits the Gospel to those only who are alive to their ruined plight. The note of warning for the unbelieving and the impenitent did not get its own place, and no more did the wooing note that sought to win the sinner to the obedience of faith. The outcome of this kind of preaching was that the eye of the hearer was directed to the hidden man of the heart to the obscuring of the call to look out and away from self to the Saviour. It is not in self in any shape or form that we can find the fullness or the help or the life that we need. It is in the fullness of the Saviour that there is a supply for all the sinner's need, and the hearer of the Gospel has to learn to put forth the faith, that goes out to Christ, for all that will meet his need, and that looks away from everyone else as a source of help and hope. Unbalanced preaching of a closed system thrust to one side the lesson taught by the looking of the dying Israelite to the brazen serpent, though such a look was the one way of cure for him in whose veins the poison of sin was working out death. In other words, an unduly introspective and one-sided presentation of the truth that bears on the enjoyment of God's favour took the place of the free, if also the one-sided, message of the early Reformers. This earlier Reformed message bore witness to Christ in His fullness and freeness, and bade the hearers take Him as their own and live in the happy confidence that He was theirs, and that in Him they had life and salvation. A kind of preaching that side-tracked the Evangel and fenced and hedged with elaborate restrictions and conditions the enjoyment of God's free salvation was one that, like Hagar, gendered to bondage."

These words express the Scriptural genuineness of God's sincere offer of salvation to all men. They speak of how deeply man's destiny is involved in the kind of response he gives to God's welcoming voice. They show that every pillow, which by way of excuse we put under our heads, is taken away. They teach us also that since God's call is personal it is never addressed to 'them' but always to 'me'. On this point there is an impressive story told about the famous Henry Moor- house who was once the guest of a wealthy gentleman in America. The story is entitled 'Finger Points To Heaven'.

This gentleman had a daughter just advancing into womanhood, and looking forward with bright anticipation to a gay and worldly life. One day she entered the library, and found the evangelist poring over his Bible. Begging pardon for the intrusion, she was about to retire when he looked up and said in his quiet and tender way, 'Are you saved?' She could only reply, 'No, Mr. Moorhouse, I am not.' Then came another question, 'Would you like to be saved?' She thought for a moment of all that is meant by salvation, and of all that is meant by the lack of salvation, and she frankly answered, 'Yes, I wish I were a sincere Christian'.

Then came the third question, asked very solemnly and earnestly, 'Would you like to be saved now?' Upon this searching thrust, her head dropped and she began to look into her heart. On one hand wealth and position in society made the world peculiarly attractive; and on the other hand stood the Lord Jesus Christ, who must then and there be received or rejected. No wonder the struggle in her breast was severe, but as the realities of eternity swept before her vision, she raised her eyes and calmly, resolutely said, 'Yes, I want to be saved now'. The supreme moment in her history was reached, and the evangelist was led by the Holy Spirit to guide her wisely.

He asked her to kneel beside him and to read aloud the 53rd Chapter of *Isaiah*. This she did in tones that became tremulous and broken by sobs. 'Read it again', said Henry, 'and wherever you find 'we', 'our' and 'us' put in 'I', 'my' and 'me'. Read it as if you were pouring out your heart before God. The weeping girl again read, "He is despised and rejected of men; a man of sorrows, and acquainted with grief; and I hid as it were my face from him; he was despised and I esteemed him not. Surely he hath borne my griefs, and carried my sorrows; yet I did esteem him stricken, smitten of God, and afflicted." Here she broke down completely, as the thought of her personal relations to the Lord Jesus in His sufferings for the first time flashed into her mind.

Then she read on: "He was wounded for my transgressions, He was bruised for my iniquities; the chastisement of my peace was upon Him; and with His stripes I am healed. I, like a sheep, have gone astray; I have turned to my own way; and the Lord hath laid on Him all of my iniquities." She was silent for a moment, and then exclaimed with deep emotion, 'Oh, Mr. Moorhouse, is this true?' 'Dear child', he answered, 'does not God say it?' Again she was silent for a time, but at length looking up, no longer through the tears of bitter grief, but in joy, and adoring gratitude, she said, 'Then I am saved, for all my iniquities have been laid on Him.'

She arose from her knees with the peace of God that passes all understanding guarding her heart and mind.

The writer of this story concludes with the words, "It is not enough to know that Christ died for many, but to believe in the heart that He died for me in particular. I must see Him by faith hanging from the Cross for my sins, suffering in my stead, taking my place under the curse of God's broken law, making my atonement with His precious blood for my soul, before I can enter into the gladness of knowing that there is therefore now no condemnation to them which are in Christ Jesus. (*Rom.* 8. 1) There are many who believe that the Bible is true, that they are sinners, and that Christ is the only Saviour, and yet fail to receive salvation because they do not put in 'I', 'my' and 'me' while reading sacred Scriptures."

Not only does the voice of the Bride reach us through the Gospel, as it is written and proclaimed, but we may hear it also in other ways. The well-known minister J. P. Struthers, of Greenock, once interviewed a young woman who desired to sit at the Lord's table. It happened that some time before then her sister had died, and at her funeral they sang a Psalm:

She shall be brought unto the King
In robes with needle wrought;
Her fellow-virgins following
Shall unto thee be brought.

Her beloved sister, she reflected, had passed within the veil. She was now without fault before the throne, and clad in the garments of righteousness, immortality and eternal joy. By

God's grace she also would become a follower of the Lord and of those 'who through faith and patience inherit the promises'. God spoke to her heart through the death of a sister and led her to seek and find salvation in His Son.

And so we end, by reminding ourselves that however God's voice reaches us, our eternal destiny is very deeply involved in whether we truly say Yes or No to His call.

12

Tramps or Travellers

The moment Rebecca made her decision to leave her father's house she became a traveller to another country. The way before her was long and arduous but her heart was set on reaching her goal. She knew that beyond the earthly journey she was also, by God's higher call, on a spiritual pilgrimage to the heavenly world. Therefore, her life was now guided by the fixed star of a higher purpose. That was inherent in her faith.

Part of the land through which Rebecca journeyed, along the fringe of the Syrian desert, was the haunt of many aimless wanderers. Many lived a nomadic life there, ever looking for some pleasant spot where to pitch their tents for a while. There also some loitered, beguiled by those mirages which so often tantalise the unwary. Rebecca might have seen those little oases, and those illusions which as the prophet tells us, so much resemble 'pools of water'. But the land of her desire lay beyond the great waste. And for her there was no tarrying.

As of old, the Arab still wanders in the desert. And figuratively speaking, so do many others besides. The world we live in, as our Lord reminds us, is indeed a desert place. Here many wander without aim or hope, intrigued by false dreams and ever looking for that elusive place or thing which may yield a momentary pleasure. Many live with no worthy end in view, unaware that they were created to travel in God's way that in so doing they might at last enjoy Him for ever. But alas, man who was made to travel in God's path has become an aimless wanderer. Like another, he pitches his tent toward a city which is destined to destruction.

It is not so long since some preached that our world was to become a paradise. Man himself was to change it into a place of rest and safety. But how suddenly has this fond dream faded.

The brave new world of our dreams is now a place of violent storms and unpredictable perils. Many are in the grip of fear. We want to escape somewhere —'away from it all'. Many would fain leave this world for another and a safer place. A physical journey to a distant star might relieve the insufferable tension of living in a cataclysmic age and world. Yet few seem to know that what we are trying to escape from is ourselves, and that even if it were possible for us to leap into another world we would still have to reckon with our own sin and conscience, with fear and with God and His inescapable judgment. In the words of a famous poet, 'We can leave everything and everybody except ourselves'. A mere physical leap out of our imperilled world into another would leave us exactly where we are and as we are. There is only one hope for us! There is only one way in which we can be rescued from our sad plight. It is that we leap out of ourselves into the safety which is in Christ and within His Kingdom.

Supposing we were told of a happy world somewhere beyond this universe, we could only wistfully sigh, knowing that we could never get there. The way is inconceivably long and we are not sure in what direction it lies. And even supposing God had provided a way into that far-off world we could still only dream of it, if we were so enfeebled and helpless that we could not possibly take the journey there.

Now the wonderful thing is that beyond this universe there is such a world. Not only so; but God has also provided a way that unerringly leads to it. And there are those, once powerless and helpless, to whom He has given the power to travel thither and who know that they are going to arrive there without fail. This is not a theological dream but a glorious reality. Indeed, it is something which happens when we entrust our souls to Christ. Listen to the words of Jesus Christ. 'I am the way, the truth and the life.' He might have said in other words, 'I, in myself, am heaven. I am the way there, and I am the life to enable men to reach that blessed place.' These are high but sound claims which have been verified in the experience of countless men and women. It happens every day.

We mentioned already how the offices of Christ as Prophet, Priest and King stand related to our eternal salvation. He is the King whose kingdom is 'full of glory' and where the inhabitant shall never say, 'I am sick'. He is the great High Priest who, through the shedding of His blood and His death on the Cross, opened a pathway for us into that lovely world. He is that safe and golden ladder which God let down from that perfect world into ours that we may travel thither. He is also the Prophet by whose life-giving word the dead are quickened and endued with unfailing life and power to enable them to reach the heavenly country. 'They shall run, and not be weary; and they shall walk, and not faint.' Christ is therefore 'the power of God and the wisdom of God'. He calls Himself the true end or the 'good part.' He is the way, and the life He gives is as empowering as it is eternal.

In contrast to this sure and perfect way of salvation 'the wisdom of this world' is seen in all its wearisome and empty characteristics. Human systems of thought often present us with some hypothetical end to live for, some ideal to aim at, or something high and noble which we 'ought' to follow. But we perish on the rock of human helplessness and our unconscious antagonism to the very ideals which we profess to admire. There is no way to translate these ideals into reality. We have no moral or spiritual power to reach the goal. This is the persistent predicament of all moral theory. It is ever bedevilled by our inability and sin. What we ought to do, we cannot do. This is a form of despair from which the true Christian is set free. It was Paul who said, 'The good that I would I cannot do because evil is present within me.' But with the next breath, and as a new man in Christ, he could 'thank God through Jesus Christ our Lord'.

And why did he, in this particular context, so fervently thank God? It is because he knew that by a continual work of grace the law of sin which warred in his members and which so often arrested his spiritual progress must yield to the greater power of God working in his heart. He knew that as his justification through Christ's righteousness was an accomplished fact, his sanctification would reach the same level of perfection. 'He which hath begun a good work in you will perform it until the day of Jesus Christ.' Of himself and of all who stand in this grace he could say —'We are more than conquerors through Him that loved us.' We are, in other words, going to arrive. 'They go from strength, every one of them in Zion appears before God.'

13

"I being in the Way"

AT this point a very important question confronts us. It is this. Are there undoubted proofs in our life that we have answered His call and that we are now travelling towards the heavenly Canaan 'in the footsteps of the flock' and are 'followers of them who through faith and patience inherit the promises'? The proofs that might be given are, indeed, so numerous that we can only mention the more obvious. But these, on the other hand, are the authentic evidence of our spiritual life.

For one thing, as soon as we obey God's call from the heart we begin to move further and further away from the world and its ways. Marriage involves a separation, and this is as true in the spiritual sphere as it is in the natural. Christ came down into our world that His Bride might follow Him to His Heavenly Home. In Psalm Forty-five He calls her out of her father's house and from among her people. She was to bid a willing and everlasting farewell to everything that had formerly claimed her heart. Both Christ and the Church came under this law of separation. But here we can only think of this separation as it is seen in the lives of God's people.

In the portion of the Word from which our story is taken a remarkable incident is recorded. It is when the servant said to Abraham, "Peradventure the woman will not be willing to follow me into this land: must I needs bring thy son again into the land from whence you came?" The answer given is not only very significant but most solemn and awe-inspiring as to its warning and its emphasis: 'Beware thou that thou bring not my son thither again'. These words plainly show not only that God's call is holy and heavenward, but that the Christian life necessarily involves us in a separation from the unfruitful works of darkness and from those who engage in them. It was so with

Abraham himself. God had called him out of Ur into another country which he was to inherit. Out of that idolatrous land he was called to serve the living God. And to that land he never went back, although the opportunity to do so was always there. Nor would he suffer even the shadow of that land to fall on his son's soul. This is one of the laws which govern God's kingdom.

In a literal sense we continue to live in the world, although not of the world and certainly not like the world. We continue to associate with our fellow men, to love and to serve and to pray for those who are still out of Christ; but our personal lives stand out in utter contrast to all that the world stands for. 'They are not of the world, even as I am not of the world.' Christ's Bride, called out of the world, refuses to conform to its pattern or to defile her garments by adapting herself to its ways. Christ cannot be 'brought down' to the level of our sinful ways. If we imagine that He can, our disillusionment will one day be complete and our presumption will fill us with dread and dismay.

In these days we hear a great deal as to what a 'Christian' may do and still remain a 'Christian'. 'Surely', it is often said, 'one can be a Christian and . . . ' Then follows a nauseating enumeration of all the things 'a Christian' may legitimately do. May 'a Christian' not dance, drink, gamble, and even play a 'harmless' game on the Lord's Day? A clean break from such things is only for the narrow-minded and the bigot! Surely we can get to Heaven though our feet tarry in the broad way and though we embrace our little idols?

But real Christians never speak or act in this way. Those who do such things are not the Lord's people. They have never left their sinful environment and associations to follow Christ. Like water they never rise above their own level. They repudiate the fundamental law of true discipleship. The Christian life must be lived in the higher dimension of a willing consecration of oneself to Christ. 'If any man will come after me, let him deny himself, and take up his cross, and follow me.' He sanctified Himself for our sake, and for His sake we dedicate our lives and persons to Him, 'which is our reasonable service'.

We once knew two ladies who lived together in a Highland glen. They lived affectionately on the same hearth, but spiritually they were far apart. 'We should walk with the times' was the pat, thoughtless phrase often on the lips of the younger woman. But the other would remind her that all true believers in Christ walked not with the 'times' but with God and according to His Word. If there is no separation from 'the world' God is not our Father and Christ is not our heavenly husband. "Wherefore come out from among them, and be ye separate . . . and I will be a Father unto you, and ye shall be my sons and daughters", says the Lord Almighty." The pilgrim to Heaven has therefore his back to the world.

Another and a very genuine proof of discipleship is this. Those who are being prepared by God for Heaven are also preparing themselves. Someone once expressed this by saying that the Church of Christ goes to Heaven on her knees. In other words, she is praying without ceasing that God might create within her a clean heart and renew and sanctify her life. She is always at the mirror of His Word, and in discovering the stains which still disfigure and mar her life, she resorts in prayer to the precious fountain of the blood of atonement where she receives cleansing and where her sins are removed and forgiven. The glorious prospect of appearing before God in Zion gives her these constant exercises of soul. 'The marriage of the Lamb is come, and His wife hath made herself ready.' She knows that without holiness no man can see the Lord. No preparation is required for a lost eternity. To enter that place of despair all that is needed is that we stay as we are and where we are.

The enjoyment of God's presence here is another sure evidence that we are in God's way. 'I being in the way, the Lord led me.' The One who so unerringly guided the servant in the way was not a mere angel but God Himself. But the Word makes it clear that this guidance was intimately linked to a holy converse with God in prayer. And true prayer ever carries with it the seal of its own genuineness and the evidence of God's companionship. There are many prayers that are still-born.

Like the formalist in the temple the 'speaking' is all on man's side, and there is no answer from God. In this way many, who may be far off from God, presume that He is with them. But those whose lives are governed by His Word hear His voice and are blessed by His presence. These also hear His voice speaking to them through the written Word and in the events of His providence. Enoch 'walked with God'. And he went to Heaven in conscious enjoyment of God as his Companion.

In *Genesis* Chapter Twenty-five we are provided with one great evidence that Rebecca also lived this life of habitual communion with God. In her new home we find her on her knees in prayer and asking God a question with regard to her children. Her prayer, along with God's immediate answer, shows that she had God's secret and the knowledge of His covenant. She was truly united to Christ, for she had His presence with her in the house of her pilgrimage.

A Christian man was walking along the road one day in one of the Highland straths. In the way two of his erstwhile companions met him and for reasons of their own passed him by without any sign of recognition. Afterwards as he rested in the house of a friend, he invoked a blessing on God's temporal gifts. It was a quotation from a Psalm.

Nevertheless continually,
O Lord, I am with thee:
Thou dost me hold by my right hand,
And still upholdest me.

By these words he meant that although men might disown him God was consciously with him and he was with God. There is, indeed, a sense in which the traveller to heaven is there already and this is one of the sweet paradoxes of the Christian life. We are there not only in God's promise and representatively in Christ, but also in our desires and enjoyments. Paul was in the highest heaven with God while he was still running towards it. Thomas Goodwin remarks that the beginnings of heaven are found in these words, 'Truly our fellowship is with the Father, and with His Son Jesus Christ'. And that is how Jacob described his blissful consciousness of God's presence at Bethel, in the words, 'This is none other but the house of God, and this is the gate of heaven.' A state of grace is therefore, potentially, a state of glory. Those in whose heart heaven is shall one day be in the heart of heaven. When we are born from above we have a place in God's family, and this is not a future hope but a present privilege and enjoyment. 'Now are we the sons of God.' Heaven is not therefore a remote abstraction or a cold ideal. 'Ye are come unto Mount Zion, and unto the city of the living God.' It is here with us as we move on to enjoy it.

Mr. C. H. Spurgeon tells of a shepherd who was once questioned by a friend concerning his assurance of salvation. The simple-minded but godly man ended his remarks by saying, 'Here Christ is with me, and in heaven I shall be with Him'. This saying is consistent with Christian experience and Christian hope in every age.

Still another proof of being in the way is an ever-increasing humility in the sight of God. This is a grace which shows itself more and more the nearer we get to God, and the more we think of His sovereign love in calling us out of darkness into His marvellous light. It was at the end of her journey that Rebecca bowed her head and, in the presence of the man who had honoured her so greatly, covered her face with a veil. In the life of the Apostle Paul we see a progressive deepening of his Christian humility as he moves toward heaven. When he thought of his calling within the highest circle of God's chosen apostles he could not but bow his head and say, 'I am not meet to be called an apostle'. Then came a stage when he saw himself as 'the least' among the great company of all believers. But it was when he was on the threshold of glory that he wrote the words, "This is a faithful saying, and worthy of all acceptation that Christ Jesus came into the world to save sinners; of whom I am the chief." It may not be too much to say that this is an holy attitude to God which shall continue to deepen throughout

Eternity. There our eyes rest for ever on Christ. There we cast our crowns at His feet and say 'Worthy is the Lamb that was slain'. *'The Lord* be magnified.'

A man was once walking along a quiet country road near the Cromarty Firth in Ross-shire. It was a lovely day in the late summer. Nature had clothed the landscape in her finest robe. Hard by the wayside lay the fringe of a very large field of corn. As he stood surveying it he saw that the corn which grew round the outer edge was so very small as to be almost unseen. It could not compare in size or strength with that which grew out in the middle of the field. And yet the small blades which had barely struggled out of the soil belonged to the field. They would be part of the harvest which would be gathered in in due time. "If", he thought, "I belonged to Christ's field, though the last and the least of that blessed number that shall finally be gathered to Him, I should be happy, happy, happy. O! to be within the circle of His covenant love, and to be among those who shall see His face with joy —though the last and the least among them." This was how he felt.

When sin entered the world it said to man 'You shall be as gods'. But when grace enters our heart we say, 'He must increase, but I must decrease,'

Another, and perhaps the greatest, proof of our being in the way is that we love Him who first loved us. Our love for Christ has a beginning but it shall have no end. He is the Lover of our soul. The hope of heaven is, therefore, the hope of being with Christ. Without Him, even Heaven itself with all its glories would be to His Bride a place of sorrow and loneliness. In that blessed abode nothing would compensate for His absence. Those who would be satisfied with a Christ- less heaven shall never be in heaven.

Let me illustrate this truth. There was a young woman who once looked forward to a happy life with the man who had given her his promise to be hers, and who had so deeply commanded her affections. But one day the shattering word reached her that all was over. He had broken his promise. He had left her for ever. Her fond dream faded out in sorrow. Her bright sky became shrouded in a perpetual twilight. A curtain of gloom, which nothing could lift, descended on her spirit. A lovely home, riches and entertainment failed to compensate for the void in her heart. Her crucified affections left her stricken all her days. And whatever favours were showered upon her, her heart remained empty and broken till death at length touched her eyes in a last long sleep.

And were Christ not in heaven, all its glories, treasures and blessings could not compensate for His absence. His Bride would still be weeping with the cry of pain on her lips: 'Have you seen Him whom my soul loves?' Of course this cannot happen; but these remarks must be made to warn those who imagine that they may enter heaven without a saving knowledge of the Redeemer and therefore without any love for Him. As the eyes of Christ's Bride are toward heaven, her heart at the same time is whispering —'Whom have I in heaven, but Thee? and there is none upon earth that I desire beside Thee'.

We believe that as Rebecca travelled towards her future homeland the servant and his companions had much to tell her of the blessings and privileges that were in store for her there. In other words, Christian fellowship on the way to heaven is a sweet thing, and is an evidence that we have passed from death to life. We are not only God's companions, but the companions of all those who love Him. Bunyan's pilgrims were always talking about the 'Lord of the hill' and of Mount Zion, their future home with God. "Then they that feared the Lord spoke often one to another: and the Lord hearkened, and heard it, and a book of remembrance was written before Him for them that feared the Lord, and that thought upon His name. And they shall be mine, says the Lord of hosts, in that day when I make up my jewels."

Perhaps, however, the most impressive proof that we are in the way is that, by God's grace, we endure and persevere to the end. We meet with much to divert our eyes and to retard our progress. We also meet with many trials and difficulties, some of which threaten to overcome us. Many set out in this way but they fail to persevere. They make shipwreck of their faith on their first contact with adversity. Others perish on the soft sands of earthly prosperity. But 'the righteous shall hold on his way', ever praying for the grace to enable them to reach the journey's end. Well does David express this in his prayer:

> Hold up my goings, Lord, me guide
> In those thy paths divine,
> So that my footsteps may not slide
> Out of those ways of Thine.

We do not know how it fared with Rebecca in her journey, but we do know that she arrived safely at last. And Christ's Bride, leaning on her Beloved, keeps on in His way 'until the day dawn, and the day-star arise in her heart'.

> Midst the light, and peace and glory
> Of the Father's home;
> Christ for me is watching, waiting,
> Waiting till I come.

> There amidst the love and glory
> He is waiting yet;
> In his hands a name is graven
> He can ne'er forget.

> There amidst the Songs of heaven
> Sweeter to his ear
> Is the footfall through the desert
> Ever drawing near.

> He and I in that bright glory
> One deep joy shall share –
> Mine to be forever with Him
> His, that I am there.

14

"A Great Wonder in Heaven"

IN some Eastern communities it was a custom that immediately after a man had married he left his bride for a season in her own home and country —just where she was. He then went back to his own land and home to prepare a place for her. And in due season he returned and brought her to his own home. This ancient custom is, we think, the social background of our Lord's great promise to His people.

He left His Bride here for 'a little while'. She is still to tarry for a brief season in that same world out of which He has redeemed her. But this hour of waiting is brief. Therefore He says, "Let not your heart be troubled . . . in my Father's house are many mansions . . . I go to prepare a place for you. And if I go and prepare a place for you, I will come again, and receive you unto myself; that where I am, there ye may be also." (*John* 14).

Christ in Heaven is, therefore, concerned with the homecoming of His people. With joy He anticipates the day when He shall present them to Himself. On earth He prayed "Father, I will that they also, whom You have given me, be with me where I am; that they may behold my glory, which Thou hast given me: for You loved me before the foundation of the world." (*John* 17).

The Apostle John, in prophetic vision, saw the Church in heaven as 'a great wonder'. "And there appeared a great wonder in heaven, a woman clothed with the sun, and the moon under her feet, and upon her head a crown of twelve stars." (*Rev.* 12) Her exaltation and glorification were to him a surpassing marvel of God's love and grace. It was a state and a change which passed beyond the bounds of recognition. Among the great multitude he saw in Heaven there were, no doubt, some who had been his 'companions in tribulation' on earth; but their glory was such that he could only ask the question: 'What are these which are arrayed in white robes and whence came they?' It was this unspeakable glorious view of their state in Heaven which made him write, "It doth not yet appear, what we shall be: but we know that, when He shall appear, we shall be like Him; for we shall see Him as He is." Scripture everywhere implies that in Heaven we shall know one another; but the change from a state of grace and suffering into a state of glory and perfect peace is so inconceivably great that even a glimpse of it from this side overwhelms us with the sheer wonder of it.

There is a story from the annals of a bygone age of a poor man who had lived all his days in obscurity. In the country to which he belonged the throne had become vacant. The king who was the last known link in the royal succession had just died. After much searching it was discovered that, by a remote and involved relationship, this poor man was of nearer kinship to the departed prince than any other. He was, therefore, immediately owned as king and lifted out of his mean circumstances into a place of supreme honour. On the day of his coronation a companion of his former days said to him, 'I would hardly know you now!' The answer was, O! I hardly know myself'. How beautifully does David express this change in the Psalm.

He from the dust doth raise the poor,
That very low doth lie;
And from the dunghill lifts the man
Oppressed with poverty:
That He may highly him advance,
And with the princes set;
With those that of his people are
The chief, ev'n princes great. (Ps. 113)

Even on earth the privilege of being admitted into God's fellowship and favour fills us with joy unspeakable. When Bunyan's Christian awoke out of his blissful sleep in the chamber called Peace he could only exclaim:

Where am I now? Is this the love and care
Of Jesus, for the men that pilgrims are?
Thus to provide that I should be forgiven,
And dwell already the next door to Heaven!

And when from this 'next door' we pass through the gates into the Lord's presence our happiness and peace shall reach their highest pinnacle of perfection.

The figures which are used in this passage from the book of *Revelation* are meant to describe the loveliness of the Church in her heavenly home. They are borrowed from the fairest scenes of Creation. Sun, moon and stars are brought together to give some conception of her beauty there. Christ, the Sun of Righteousness, adorns her person and warms her heart. The shadows have fled away, for there is no night there. The sun, risen upon her, shall no more go down. The moon, the symbol of her former night and of earth's dimmer dispensation, is under her feet. She has now emerged out of her low estate and darkness into a dimension of unfading glory and life. Her brow is bejewelled with stars — stars which she won for her Lord. But that crown she shall lay at His feet who alone is worthy of her adoration. "Worthy is the Lamb that was slain to receive power, and riches, and wisdom, and strength, and honour, and glory, and blessing." The seven jewels of praise mentioned in this verse the saints shall bring before Christ for ever. The Church, through her travail and ministry in this world, is the means of bringing many souls to her Lord, but the glory of all her labour shall redound to His own praise.

If her transformation is 'a great wonder', so also is her preservation. Like her Lord, she was on earth the object of the devil's malice and of men's hatred. And who can know 'the depths of Satan'? The final triumph of the Church is 'a great wonder' of God's providence and of God's power. 'Almost they consumed me on the earth.' But 'they overcame through the blood of the Lamb and the word of His testimony'.

No doubt as God's people look back on the path that they

had to traverse through life's 'great and terrible wilderness' they will say with Bunyan's Pilgrim as he surveyed his perilous passage through the Valley of the Shadow of Death:

O world of wonders! (I can say no less),
That I should be preserv'd in that distress
That I have met with here! O blessed be
That hand that from it hath deliver'd me!
Dangers in darkness, devils, hell, and sin,
Did compass me while I this vale was in:
Yea, snares, and pits, and traps, and nets did lie
My path about, that worthless silly I
Might have been catch'd, entangled, and cast down:
But since I lived, let Jesus wear the crown.

Many of God's people while they rejoice in the hope of heaven dread the last dark vale which separates time from eternity. The implications of physical death are so awe-inspiring that some of God's choicest saints have trembled as they saw eternity come into view, and time, with its irrevocable opportunities and persistent neglects, coming to a final end.

We believe, however, that 'dying in the Lord' has deeper consolations than anything we have known or enjoyed in this life. He is very near to us then. 'When you pass through the waters, I shall be with you.' He went this way Himself, and He knows how to comfort us as Death beckons us away. Besides, our translation from these broken scenes into God's presence only takes a moment. 'Absent from the body, present with the Lord.' It was God's promise to David that dissolved his fear of the valley of the shadow of death. 'I shall fear no evil, for Thou art with me.' Death cannot harm us since Christ endured its sting. In this way He deprived it of its power and ability to hurt us.

Sometimes as we stand by the beds of our dying Christian friends we may infer how great is their happiness as they move away from us. Some of them are able to tell us a little of what they feel and see as their souls stand on the threshold of glory.

Let me give an example: just one out of many. Many years ago a young woman entered a church in her native Lochaber. Her name was Margaret MacKinnon. The minister, the Rev. Donald MacFarlane, read his text which was from the Prophecy of *Jeremiah*. "O! Hope of Israel, the Saviour thereof in time of trouble, why should You be a stranger in the land, or as a wayfaring man that turns aside to tarry for a night?" As these words were read, her heart was deeply touched. That day marked her spiritual rebirth. God took possession of her soul, and from that hour she also became a wayfarer on earth, seeking 'the city that hath foundations', and no longer a stranger to God.

Shortly afterwards in the town of Inverness she entered a church. The congregation were singing a Psalm which, in her experience at least, instantly transformed the place into a Bethel. The words sung were:

God is of mine inheritance
And cup the portion.
The lot that fallen is to me
Thou dost maintain alone.

God's love flooded her soul, and for a season she walked in the light of His face. God, indeed, was preparing her for heaven. Within a few months she took ill. But as death approached, her soul was wrapped up in unspeakable joy. On the day on which she died it was light at eventide. 'Oh!' she exclaimed, 'I have much joy', and a little later she cried again —'My joy is increasing! Do you see the angels?' She said after a while —'I see them. They are very many and their robes are shining white.' Then she asked the time and on being told, she replied —'In half an hour I shall join the angels. They are waiting for me with a smile on their faces.' In exactly half an hour she peacefully breathed her last.

Even when Death comes suddenly and in the garments of terror we may, as in the case of Stephen, be instantly delivered from all fear in finding ourselves standing, with eyes unveiled, on the threshold of the world of glory.

On a dark New Year's Day morning in 1919 a ship, carrying hundreds of sailors to their Hebridean homes, struck a treacherous rock and sank. Two lads were struggling in the waves. 'We are going down', said the one to his friend. The other —an excellent Christian boy— replied, 'No; I am going up'. Having said that. a huge wave passed over his head and he was seen no more. His companion survived to tell the story to his loved ones.

Some of God's people, we know, die with their lips sealed. They pass out in silence and in the stillness of their last sleep. God would have it so. But the same joy and ministry await all who love Him. The moment Christ, the Beloved, draws the curtain which separates time from eternity we stand in His blissful presence. We are Home. It is good, therefore, to wait for the salvation of the Lord, till the day of trial is over and we hear His welcoming voice: 'Arise my love, my fair one, and come away'.

If, as Sir Herbert Grierson believed, the story of Rebecca's wooing, her long pilgrimage to the land where her husband dwelt, and her final joy in seeing face to face the one whom she had not seen and yet loved is, in the realm of literature, one of the loveliest stories ever penned on earth; on the other hand the loveliest story that has been proclaimed on earth and which shall be celebrated in the songs of the Redeemed in Heaven is the story of Christ's love for His Bride and the everlasting bliss of those who answer 'I will' to His call.

15

The Servant's Joy

IF at the end of his days someone had asked Abraham's servant what was the event in his life which had given him the greatest satisfaction and joy, he might have replied that it was that memorable morning when Bethuel's daughter consented to leave her father's house and to become the wife of his master's son. As a man of prayer who enjoyed much nearness to God, he knew that beyond the mere setting of that event higher issues were involved. His was the joy of knowing that he was the means of bringing her into the family of him who had the promise of a great spiritual inheritance in which she was also to share.

Suppose that in the same way one were to ask a true servant of the Lord the question, 'What is the end of all your labour and what is it that you desire above all things in this life?' Would he not answer, 'It is that I might be used of the Holy Spirit to lead someone to Christ'? To be the means of bringing even one soul to Christ is the greatest achievement and joy that can come the way of anyone in this world. It is a greater achievement than if we should make the very stars our stepping stones to encompass all Creation. God gives the highest commendation and the greatest promise to the one who labours to rescue others from eternal death. 'He that wins souls is wise.' 'Well done, thou good and faithful servant . . . enter thou into the joy of thy Lord.'

Paul speaks of his many converts as his 'joy and crown' in the day of Christ.

When as a young man the much-loved Bishop Taylor Smith had heard how God had blessed his message in the conversion of a sinner he bowed his head and whispered — 'Lord, now let your servant depart in peace; for my eyes have seen Your salvation'. There is a depth in this joy known only to those who have tasted it.

A minister of Christ once spoke in public on 'the sorrows of the preacher'. He mentioned the sorrow which a cold indifferent attitude to the Gospel invitation produces in the heart of a man who over the years proclaims the 'good news' to his congregation. After the service and as he was moving away from the Church, a young man walked toward him. "A little while ago," this lad said, "you preached a sermon which was, I hope, the means of leading me to Christ. Perhaps after all, your labour is not in vain." That evening as this man journeyed home alone, a wonderful joy began to well up in his heart. He then knew, in some measure at least, the joy which is in the presence of the angels over one sinner who repents and returns.

'With what word would you like to close your eyes at last in this world?' This was the somewhat startling question which a preacher of the Gospel once asked another. The one who asked the question said, 'I would like to die with the words of Abraham's servant on my lips: "Let me go; for the Lord hath prospered my journey"'. After a moment of silence the other replied: 'And I, too, would like to die with these same words'. How well do the words of Samuel Rutherford express this yearning which is in the heart of every true preacher of God.

> Fair Anwoth by the Solway,
>   To me thou still art dear!
> Even from the verge of Heaven
>   I drop for thee a tear.
> Oh! if one soul from Anwoth
>   Meet me at God's right hand
> My Heaven will be two Heavens
>   In Immanuel's land.

The excellent Rev. John Anderson who laboured in the Gospel in various parts of Canada was wafted into Heaven on a wave of joy. Sometime before he died a dark cloud overshadowed this spirit; but as 'the dawn of heaven' began to break in upon his soul he began to clasp his hands. "It is all right now," he said, "They say a drowning man sees all his life pass before him in a moment of time, and I, too, have had such a vision. The Good Master has spread out before me all I have ever tried to do for Him, and the sky is full of stars —stars which I have won for Him. I can see where they begin, but I cannot see where they end." The thought that he had been the means of winning souls for his master's crown filled him with the deepest joy. The 'stars' were with him to the end, and the words 'happy, happy' lingered on his lips till he passed into God's presence.

There is no sorrow of any kind in heaven; but the prospect of entering it without some token of our diligence and zeal is not a happy one. The joy of heaven is intimately associated with the improvement of our time and talents here in the service of the Lord. Time is short. Our talents may be few. But the Lord commands us to redeem the time, and to use our gifts in His service. The welcome into the joy of the Lord is extended to those who have put their time and gifts to good use.

A noted preacher once had a strange dream. He saw himself entering heaven, the door of which was wide open to welcome him. At the door stood his Lord whose face, for some reason, bore a look of displeasure. This gave him much concern. As he was about to cross the threshold of that blessed world the Lord asked him to look behind him. He did so and saw that he had come alone. There was no one behind him. He had brought none with him. When he awoke he made haste to work and to pray that he might still be used of God in the salvation of souls. God owned his labours, and at the end of the day he entered his Master's presence bringing with him many tokens of a rich spiritual harvest. It is therefore true that 'heaven will be two heavens' if there we meet those who, through our prayers, example or exhortation turned to the Lord.

Those who wrestle with God for the conversion of souls, and who plead with men to be reconciled to God are given a promise, the far-reaching implications of which we cannot understand here. 'And they that be wise shall shine as the brightness of the firmament; and they that turn many to righteousness as the stars for ever and ever.'

And may those who read this book, and I who have tried to tell a little of what God has done, meet together in that better world of love, of bliss and song, 'with Christ, which is far better'.

Then those who sow and those who reap shall rejoice together.

Biographical note

The Revd Murdoch Campbell (1900-1974) was born in Swainbost on the Island of Lewis; his father was a crofter fisherman and missionary. He attended the village school until he was twelve, saw military service in 1918, and was apprenticed as a shipwright in Greenock. At the age of twenty-two he began his studies at Skerry's College, going on to graduate from Edinburgh University and then to study at the Free Church of Scotland College (now the Edinburgh Theological Seminary). He married Mary Fraser, from Strathpeffer in Ross-shire. They had three surviving children: Anne Jack, Mary MacMillan and David Campbell. His ministerial charges were Fort Augustus and Glenmoriston in Inverness-shire, Partick Highland in Glasgow, and Resolis in Ross-shire. During the Second War he was Naval Chaplain at Portsmouth and Plymouth. He was Moderator of his Church in 1956. He contracted cancer, and retired in 1968.

A gifted pastor, preacher and evangelist, he also won the esteem and deep appreciation of a wide public as author of around seventeen books. These include *Memories of a Wayfaring Man* and *In All Their Affliction*, along with biography, sermons and pamphlets. More recent publications include his diary, called *The Suburbs of Heaven*, and a collection of his Gaelic hymns with translations, entitled *Tobraichean Solais* or *Wells of Joy*.

David Campbell
Editor

Publications by the Revd Murdoch Campbell, M.A. (1900-1974)

Books
God's Unsettled Controversy (London, circa 1944)
Thy Own Soul Also **or** The Crisis in the Church (Glasgow 1945)
The King's Friend (Glasgow 1946)
The Coming Storm (Glasgow 1948)
Gleanings of Highland Harvest (1953)
The Diary of Jessie Thain (1955)
The Loveliest Story Ever Told (Inverness 1962)
In All Their Affliction (Inverness 1967)
Everlasting Love: Devotional Sermons (Edinburgh: Knox Press 1968)
From Grace to Glory: Meditations on the Book of Psalms (Banner of Truth Trust 1970)
No Night There: Devotional Sermons (Stornoway 1972)
Memories of a Wayfaring Man (Inverness 1974)
Tobraichean Solais: Wells of Joy (Covenanters Press 2013)
The Suburbs of Heaven: The Diary of Murdoch Campbell (Covenanters Press 2014)

Translations
Des Konings vriend : Het leven en sterven Norman Macdonald (C. B. van Woerden Jr te Akkrum, Utrecht 1961)
Herinneringen van een Pelgrim (trs. J. Kooistra, Veenendaal 1978)
Dagboek van Jessie Thain (J. Kooistra 1980)
Nalezingen van de Highland-oogst (J. Kooistra, Gorinchem 1995)
In al hun benauwdheid: pastorale memoires van een Schotse predikant (trs. Ruth Pieterman: Gouda 2013)

Pamphlets
The Earth-bound Vision: A Critical Examination of Pre-millennialism
After Bishops – What? The New Peril
Christians and the Use of Nuclear Weapons

Tract
When my Heart Smiled

Lightning Source UK Ltd.
Milton Keynes UK
UKOW02f1603160317
296775UK00001B/228/P